TAKE ME OUT ~~TO~~ OF THE BALL GAME

TAKE ME OUT ~~TO~~ OF THE BALL GAME

Joe Campbell

thistledown press

Library and Archives Canada Cataloguing in Publication

Campbell, Joe, 1929-
Take me out of the ball game / Joe Campbell.

ISBN 1-894345-82-7

1. Canada--Humor. 2. National characteristics, Canadian--Humor. 3. Canadian wit and humor. I. Title.

PS8605.A546T33 2005 C818'.602 C2005-900885-7
Cover and book design by Jackie Forrie
Author photo by Milton Taylor
Printed and bound in Canada on acid-free paper

Thistledown Press Ltd.
633 Main Street, Saskatoon, Saskatchewan, S7H 0J8
www.thistledown.sk.ca

Canada Council for the Arts Conseil des Arts du Canada

Canadian Heritage Patrimoine canadien

Thistledown Press gratefully acknowledges the financial assistance of the Canada Council for the Arts, the Saskatchewan Arts Board, and the Government of Canada through the Book Publishing Industry Development Program for its publishing program.

ACKNOWLEDGMENTS

Although writing is solitary, publishing is collaborative. I am grateful to my collaborators, the magazine, newspaper and radio editors, who published these pieces individually, and to Thistledown Press, which is now publishing them as a collection. Thistledown's commitment to excellence was demonstrated in the choice of Don Kerr as my editor. I am grateful to Don for prompting me to make needed improvements and reminding me that brevity is the soul of wit.

CONTENTS

For Rosemary

Preface

HUMOUR IS SERIOUS STUFF. Light prose is heavy work. You need to have your wits about you to write nonsense. In "Humour as I See It," Stephen Leacock declared: "Few people realize how extremely difficult it is to tell a story so as to reproduce the real fun of it — to 'get it over' as the actors say. The mere 'facts' of a story seldom make it funny. It needs the right words, with every word in its proper place."

For most of my life, I've been a student of humourists, from Leacock to Mark Twain through Robert Benchley, James Thurber, S.J. Perelman, Eric Nicol, Norman Ward and Dave Barry, to mention a few. Good humour, I've found, is like poetry. Style and substance are inseparable. There are subsidiary meanings and effects that depend, as Leacock wrote, on the right word in its proper place and how the ideas are sequenced. To disturb any of this is to risk destroying it.

I was startled a few years ago when an editor at a news magazine reduced one of my humour pieces by a third before publishing it. "You didn't edit it," I told him in a letter of complaint. "You re-wrote it. If you were editing a poetry magazine, you wouldn't re-write someone's poem. You wouldn't, or shouldn't, even edit it without consultation. The same should go for humour."

I went on to say that if he thought my piece fell short, he should have rejected it. Like most freelance writers, I'm used to rejection. I'd prefer rejection of my humour to revision.

The editor replied pleading necessity. He graciously allowed that my piece was fine as submitted and conceded that he had done it significant violence. However, at the last minute he had a hole to fill and mine was the only usable writing in his emergency bin. Since the piece didn't fit the hole, and he had no time to consult me, he revised it "in the name of desperation, not improvement."

It was less than edifying to learn that my piece had been languishing in an emergency bin as insurance against a dreaded hole and was published out of desperation. But it was enlightening. It no doubt explains why other editors have sometimes taken brash liberties with articles I have submitted and left me wondering whether they were still mine.

Writers need editors and I have had some good ones. One of the advantages of an anthology is that writers and editors have time for leisurely consultation and articles ravaged at first publication can regain their integrity. All of the articles in this anthology were published or broadcast previously; most pretty much as they appear here, although often with different titles.

Here is where they were seen or heard. *Stitches, the Journal of Medical Humour*: "Ready Aye Ready", "Take Me Out of the Ball Game", "For Him the Bell Tolled", "Bewitched by Birders", "All You Can Eat", "A Patient's Lament", "The Theory of Devolution", "Terra Incognita", "Hearing is Believing", "One of Me is Enough", "Law and Literature", "Count Me Out", "Dingwall to the Rescue",

"Canine Capers", "Night Life", "Deal Me Out", "United We Burn", "Our Next Big Thing", "Down with Renown", and "Bowing Out"; *Gilbert Magazine*: "A Lesson in Commerce", "The War of the Words", "Father's Little Helpers", "Personality Plus", "Grave New World", "Have a Nice Day", "Exit Walking", "Commercial Art", "On with the Show", and "Modern Philosophy"; *Western People*: "Take a Bus", "Hooked on Golf", "Safaris in Suburbia", "Breakfast in Bed", "Home Cooking", and "Under the Weather and Over the Hill"; the *Toronto Star*: "How Jazz Began", Shoot the Messenger", "Looking Back", "The Irish Connection", and "What a Way to Go"; *The Globe and Mail*: "There's Something about the Irish", "All the Way to the Bank", and "My Annual Food Fight"; *Western Report*: "Hold the Phone", and "Have I Got News for You"; *Canadian Author*: "Writers versus Editors"; the *Calgary Herald*: "The Main Event"; the *Ottawa Citizen*: "School's Out"; CBC Saskatchewan: "How to Write News".

Writers versus Editors

THESE WRITERS. I don't know how they do it. I don't know how they get around editors the way they do merely by putting pen to paper or fingers to typewriter or word processor. I can't do it. I can't sell an editor a single word, let alone the thousands that professional writers put on the market daily. Yet, it's all in a day's work for them. One writer I know sells 1,000 words a week to the *Foompswitch Journal*. Imagine, 1,000 words a week. At that rate you'd think he'd have run out months ago. Another, only in the last day or so, had a call from the *Arctic Quarterly* for 5,000 words. Did it rattle him? Not at all. He had them in his head. I don't understand it. I don't think I ever will. But it never ceases to fascinate me. I'm especially fascinated with the novelists, who sell words in lots of 100,000. They say it's easier to market 100,000 words than 100. I don't see how. I don't even know 100,000 words.

What fascinates me most is the kind of money writers get. Several magazines I've read pay twenty-five cents a word. You'd think they'd offer more for proper nouns and verbs and less for prepositions and articles, but they don't. Write them a common ordinary "to" and you've earned a quarter, "a" and you've got yourself another, "the" and you've run it up to seventy-five cents. Little wonder that most writers are content with their lot. Some of the really top publications, like *McFigles*, pay a dollar a word. Then they turn around and sell the magazine for a couple of dollars a copy. Oh, I know it has to do with higher economics and all that, and I imagine there's a proper explanation somewhere, but I'm fascinated all the same. Think of it, getting a dollar for sending in an interjection like "ugh" or an interruption like "hic."

Once when I was young and confident I tried writing for the magazines. I wrote 12,000 words for *Sock*. They never replied. I wrote 6,000 words for *Screech*. They weren't interested. I wrote 3,000 words for *Shepherds Ho*. They couldn't be bothered. I wrote back offering to give them the words, all or any of them. They told me never mind. They had all they needed. The secret, of course, is to catch them when they don't have all they need. It's a matter of timing, like athletics. Some people have a nose for it. I don't have an athletic nose.

Editors normally return unwanted material with a rejection slip. All writers, no matter how illustrious, are bound to get several of these sooner or later. Dickens in the nineteenth century was rejected by *Punch* and Hemingway in the twentieth century was turned down by the *Atlantic Monthly*. So it's not something you need to keep from the neighbours or speak about in hushed tones.

The standard rejection slip is a simple form letter without salutation or signature that says something like this: "We have examined the enclosed material. However, it does not meet our current editorial requirements." Isn't that clever? They don't really reject it at all. It's just that they can't use it now. If you had sent them the piece a month earlier, or held it a month longer, they might have mailed you a fat cheque. As I said, it's a matter of timing.

The really successful authors aren't any better at writing than you or I. It's their timing that's better.

If you persist, your timing usually improves and you can expect to graduate to a personalized rejection slip. This has a salutation and a signature and the wording is more informal and varied. I received a series of these one summer from the managing editor of a national magazine. He was sitting in for the articles editor, who had taken an extended holiday. The first one went something like this: "Dear Sir: Your submission is amusing and I enjoyed reading it. However, our present editorial needs are such that we cannot use it. Regards . . . "

Thus encouraged, I sent him off another piece. "Dear Sir," he replied. "This is witty and rather well done. However . . . " If it weren't for that word "however" we'd have a great many more successful writers in this country. Anyhow, I tried again and the managing editor replied: "This is really funny and you certainly know how to write. However . . . "

I decided to try once more. By then I didn't care about getting into his magazine. I wanted to read the next rejection slip. I suspected it might say something like, "Dear Sir. This is the most hilarious piece we have ever rejected . . . " Unfortunately, the articles editor had returned to work and all I got was the standard treatment. My timing was off again.

Manuscripts submitted for publication go through a hierarchy of judges, with the rejected becoming almost unrecognizable and the accepted losing their identity entirely. If they survive the postal system, they go to the first reader, an undergraduate whose job depends on his ability to keep writers out of print. Like writers, he gets paid by the word: the more words he rejects, the more he gets paid. Whether he rejects a manuscript or passes it on for higher consideration is decided by a series of tests. The first consists in crumpling it into a ball and unravelling it. If it's still readable, he takes it to a cafe and slurps coffee over it, after which he stuffs it into his back pocket, returns with it to the office, and sits on it for the rest of the day. If it's intact when he reaches home in the evening, he stays up half the night burning holes in it with cigarettes and sprinkling it with beer.

When a submission escapes the first reader, it goes to a panel of editors for further scrutiny. This involves more cigarette burns and a sprinkling of gin. The final authority is the editor-in-chief, who butts a cigar on the title page and uses the other pages to mop up spilled Scotch.

Once a manuscript is accepted it is given to an editorial assistant whose principal job is to take out all the verbs and pass it on to a senior editor who puts in new ones. This is repeated with the other parts of speech and other assistant and senior editors and is known as editing. The last step, before the manuscript is typeset, is to change the title to suit the edited material.

Writers receive free copies of magazines in which their work appears. This allows them to become familiar with it in case their friends ask questions. Following publication, various rights revert to the author, and he may submit his work to other magazines at home or abroad. Some writers have marketed the same piece many times and then put together the different versions and sold them as a collection.

Some writers have agents, or is it the other way around? Agents know what editors want. They know when editors want what they want. They know where editors want what they want when they want it. They know how editors want what they want when and where they want it. They don't know why. Neither do the editors. Agents get their specialized knowledge in many different ways. The most popular is buying editors the cigarettes, cigars, beer, gin and Scotch with which they shower fire and firewater on manuscripts.

A Lesson in Commerce

JUNK MAIL isn't all bad. When it came time to replace our washer and dryer, I was delighted to receive an advertisement for a deluxe ensemble that featured everything we needed. I volunteered to go down and buy it.

"I want this," I said to the first salesman I saw, showing him the ad.

"Ah," he sighed, clasping his hands as though in prayer and raising his eyes toward heaven. I was somewhat taken aback. I couldn't imagine anyone getting devotional over a household appliance.

"Ah," he repeated, becoming misty eyed. "You wish to see the Domestic Angels."

"I do not," I said, "and I'm quite certain they do not wish to see me. I want to buy a washer and dryer. This one." I showed him the ad again.

"Come," the salesman said, beckoning me to follow. "Come and see." He talked and acted as though he were leading me into the antechamber of paradise. I expected to meet the firm's chaplain or its patron saint. It turned out to be only a display room with velvet upholstery and quiet lights. On a revolving dais stood the washer and dryer in the advertisement. The air was heavy with the odour of incense, and soft, inspirational music played in the background. I turned away. I was afraid I might see him genuflect.

"The Domestic Angels," he proclaimed, bowing first to the washer and then to its companion, the dryer.

"I'll take them," I said. "How much do I owe you?" Since they looked genuine, I could see no reason for haggling.

"Aren't they divine?" he said, his voice throbbing with emotion. He was clearly in ecstasy and it seemed a shame to disturb him.

"Wrap them up," I said. "Here's my address."

"Notice the chaste simplicity of design, the dazzling purity of the enamel, the seraphic richness of the chrome." He was determined to deliver his sales pitch in spite of my having decided to buy the set before leaving home.

"Observe," he said, entranced, "the new patented Chlorospray that makes clothes fresher than if they'd blown for a day on the golden prairie, or by the blue sea. Fresher than fresh is how we describe it." As he talked, he gestured reverently, walking around the Domestic Angels in a manner that suggested a sacrificial intent.

"Observe also," he continued, "the exclusive Immaculo-unit in the washer, which makes clothes cleaner than clean." The way he said it suggested that my own clothes were unclean. In a vague, yet disturbing, fashion I felt somehow inferior.

"And see the improved Dehydro-flue in the dryer. Until you've experienced it, you'll never know the thrill of wearing clothes that are really dry. It's a measure of dryness that was revealed for the first time with the advent of the Domestic Angels. They get clothes dryer than dry."

I wanted to ask, though I didn't dare interrupt again, whether the Domestic Angels were manufactured, or came into being by a special act of creation.

"No other units on the market can offer these exciting, ecstatic features, and they're only the delightful beginning. Wait 'til I tell you the glorious end." At this point he lost control and threw his arms around the dryer in a paroxysm of joy.

"The vent — it's our unique Aromahue — humidifies, deodorizes and disinfects the air while drying your clothes. Like celestial blooms, the Domestic Angels generate their own sweet perfumes, distilling fragrance throughout your home."

The feeling of inferiority was deepening. I began to wonder whether my family and I were worthy of the Domestic Angels. Just standing beside them, I felt like the publican in the temple.

"Watching them work together," he went on, "is like seeing a sunset for the first time. Introducing them into your home establishes a new dimension in cleanliness, and cleanliness, you know, is next to godliness."

This surely must have been the climax he had been building up to. I'd heard lovers talk that way about their beloved. I'd seen composers carry on like that about their music. I wondered whether he'd soon tell me that the Domestic Angels played Beethoven's *Fifth Symphony* while doing the clothes. Climax or not, he raved on.

"Look," he said, removing his shoes and climbing into the washer. "It gives a Turkish bath that would make a sultan envious. The most powerful rulers of antiquity never knew a pleasure so royal as this."

"Can they play Beethoven's *Fifth* while doing the clothes?" He was too wound up to answer.

"Your life," he said, stepping out of the Turkish bath, "will be fundamentally and irreversibly changed by the Domestic Angels. Their purchase will mean that you have unquestionably entered the world of tomorrow."

I couldn't take much more. By this time, I was stricken with guilt feelings. I didn't live in a palace, I lived in a house; I wasn't a sultan, I was a sometime writer. How could I presume to remain in the presence of the Domestic Angels, let alone desire to possess them? It was surely the height of hubris even to think of wearing clothes that were fresher than fresh, cleaner than clean, and dryer than dry. I was a mere mortal, not a Greek god.

"You'll love them," he said. "Your wife will find them irresistible. You'll both wonder how you ever managed without them."

I believed it, every word. I believed it as I'd never believed anything before. He said that I would love them, and already I was feeling more than mildly amorous. Another few minutes and, like him, I would have been singing their praises as John Keats sang the praises of nature and Francis Thompson the praises of the author of nature.

"Their arrival is the greatest event," he went on, "since the coming of the Silent Cavaliers, our new line of refrigerators." As if sensing the conflict of emotions within me, he let fall a velvet curtain that hid the Domestic Angels from view, and we were alone, the salesman and me. Like a different person, he said,

"You may pay cash, or nothing down and monthly installments."

It was a terrible position to be in, wanting them so much yet aware of my unworthiness. I resolved to do the noble thing.

"No thanks," I said. "I can't take them." It was as if I had desecrated the display room.

"You doubt their quality?" he said with an inflection that implied it was sacrilegious to harbour such thoughts.

"It's my quality I doubt," I replied as I turned to flee. "I'm not good enough for them."

I learned later that shortly afterwards he gave up his job and went into a Nestorian monastery. It was the first time his sales pitch had failed.

I wonder if he prays for me.

Ready Aye Ready

I'VE BEEN THINKING a lot lately about the Canadian military. A TV newscaster got me started after I read an account of the Canadian Coast Guard and how it protects our maritime boundaries. When I switched on the TV set, the newscaster was saying something about the Governor General's Foot Guards. I hadn't realized the Governor General's feet were being protected, too, or by whom.

It makes sense, though. Like the Queen, the Governor General goes on frequent walkabouts. There's no telling what dangers this exposes her feet to. A head of state can't be too careful about her feet. She may be only a figure head, but her feet are the real thing.

The newscaster also mentioned The Queen's Own Rifles. I was surprised to learn that she had any. I thought she was in favour of gun control. But this makes sense, too. If an intruder were to slip into Buckingham Palace unnoticed, as has already happened, the Queen should be able to protect herself. The Queen's honour is at least as important as the Governor General's feet.

My interest piqued, I skimmed a brief outline of military history and discovered that The Fort Garry Horse served in Normandy during World War II. I had assumed that by then horses no longer fought in the front lines, but I guess they still did. The Fort Garry Horse, in fact, served with The Queen's Own Rifles, which Her Majesty apparently relinquished for the duration of the war. The outline didn't explain how the army trained a horse to shoot, and I wasn't particularly concerned. Nowadays, you can teach an animal almost anything.

What interested me more is that The Fort Garry Horse went on to serve with Lord Strathcona's Horse in the Korean War. Even more remarkable, it is still in the army, although in a reserve capacity. This has to be some kind of record for equine longevity.

I was also interested in the Royal Canadian Hussars, an armoured regiment that goes back to the beginning of the nineteenth century. Well, to be honest, it doesn't really go back that far. The army hasn't yet mastered time travel. Rather, the unit has come forward this far, and it's still going strong. Hussars, I suspect, is a masculine appellation that survives from an earlier time. Today, it should be quite acceptable to call female members of the regiment hussies.

Then there are the dragoons. The Royal Canadian Dragoons have fought all over the world. They can't seem to get along with anyone. The regiment specializes in digitized operations and, in fact, leads the army in digital procedures. These are a much feared weapon.

The Saskatchewan Dragoons are a reconnaissance squadron. During advances, they check out areas ahead of the main body of troops; during withdrawals, they maintain contact with the enemy while the main body pulls back. They speak of their role as "First in-Last Out." For this reason, they are forbidden to conduct digital procedures and examinations. If they did, it would almost certainly violate the Geneva Convention.

Dragoon is obviously a corruption of dragon, a fierce fighter indeed. Some administrative flunky probably introduced the extra "o" while doodling and it survived through bureaucratic inertia.

The Queen is even more directly involved with the navy than with the army. She owns all the ships. The initials HMCS, for Her Majesty's Canadian Ship, is stamped on vessels of both the regular navy and the naval reserve. Regular navy vessels are based primarily in the coastal centres of Halifax and Esquimalt. Reserve navy ships are located in cities across Canada. When I joined a navy band in high school, I was concerned about having to rehearse at HMCS Unicorn in Saskatoon. I thought I might get seasick. I needn't have worried. To blend into the urban landscape, reserve navy ships masquerade as buildings, and rarely put out to sea.

Unlike the other services, the Canadian Air Force doesn't recruit horses or unicorns. At one time, however, it enlisted golden hawks and it still deploys snowbirds. Although these species may seem unsuitable for combat duty, they have been put to clever use. Like the Golden Hawks before them, the Snowbirds specialize in aerobatics, a diversionary tactic that confuses enemy aircraft so that our fighter planes can more easily shoot them down.

The Snowbirds are based at 15 Wing Moose Jaw. 15? It's an odd number indeed. It suggests that someone is flying on one wing. Moose Jaw? It's an odd name. They should change it to Bird Beak.

The Snowbirds are active from April through October. Although it is unclear what they do the rest of the year, they are rumoured to overwinter in California, Arizona,

Texas and other southern locales. I think they should go to Ottawa for the winter. They could help guard the Governor General's feet.

How to Write News

ANYONE WHO HAS WATCHED reporters at work must surely marvel at their speed and efficiency. I know I do. Some of the reporters I've seen can write up a fire almost as fast and efficiently as it happens; and as for traffic accidents, well, I'm not so sure that they haven't a kind of special knowledge about them before they happen. You get that impression from the matter-of-fact way they go about their work while everyone else stands around in little clumps, gaping. Nothing surprises the reporters. They knew that the accidents would happen that weekend anyhow, and some of them had already published their predictions. Their only reason for attending is to fill in the minor details, like the names of the dead and injured.

Good reporters don't get that way overnight. It sometimes takes several weeks. It takes longer if they have a university education to overcome. But once they get that way they're unmistakable. After observing scores of them, I've identified some of the questions they most often face and the answers the best of them would likely give if we called upon them to preach what they practise. If you're interested in reporting, check your own answers against these. A score of more than seventy-five percent indicates severe reportorial tendencies and suggests that you'd better see an editor right away.

Q) If you happen upon a traffic accident, what is the first thing you should do?

A) Call a photographer.

Q) What if one or more persons are injured?

A) Under no circumstances should they be moved. It might spoil the picture.

Q) What is the correct way to approach accident victims who are conscious?

A) Identify yourself and find out their names.

Q) Is there any danger in this?

A) Yes. It could result in serious complications if they give you a wrong spelling.

Q) What about next of kin?

A) Most people have them, so don't worry. If they don't find out sooner, they'll know shortly after you've released your story that there's been an accident.

Q) What is the first thing to do when the paramedics arrive?

A) Interview them.

Q) What should you look for at a political convention?

A) The bar. Sooner or later everyone of any importance will arrive there.

Q) Are all conventions alike?

A) There are two kinds of conventions: those with bars and those without. It has been found by experience that the latter are seldom newsworthy and are of limited interest to reporters.

Q) Should reporters accept drinks from anyone?

A) By all means, from everyone. Otherwise, they may be accused of discriminating.

Q) Some public figures are difficult to interview and appear reluctant to speak for publication. What is the best way to overcome their reticence?

A) Misquote them.

Q) Some people make a habit of saying they've been misquoted. How do you deal with them?

A) Quote them exactly.

Q) Some subjects like medicine and nuclear physics are highly specialized, and are difficult for lay people to comprehend. How do you write stories about these?

A) Generally with a word processor, although some news offices still use typewriters.

Q) Are certain kinds of news stories more popular than others?

A) Television producers have found that viewers prefer their fiction light. But editors have discovered that viewers and readers prefer their non-fiction dark. If you desire speedy advancement in the news business, let somebody else write the smiles and chuckles. You stay with the doom and gloom.

News gathering is but a part, and the least artistic part, of a reporter's work. Far more demanding is the writing of colourful copy under the pressure of deadlines. To do this, reporters stock their memories with words and phrases that have stood the test of time and whose intrinsic colour is beyond dispute. A really experienced reporter is a walking thesaurus. Tell him that the city hall is on fire and he can write the first three paragraphs without getting out of his chair. At the mere mention of fire, his memory erupts with such verbal fragments as holocaust, raging inferno, licked by hungry flames, braving the elements, risking life and limb. All he needs to do to complete the story is drop down to the fire for a few minutes to fill in the missing nouns and verbs.

Tell him that the nation is moving into a recession and his agile mind bubbles with such fragments as unemployment skyrocketing, retail sales softening, feeling the pinch, mass march, proposals under wraps, meetings behind closed doors, shot in the arm, wake-up call to economists, and child poverty. Knowing nothing more than the bare facts of any situation, a good reporter can take to his computer and produce a story to whatever specifications his editor prescribes.

Beginners can't do that. Beginners can collect the facts for someone else to write up, but they're not equipped to do it themselves. Only when they've built up a sufficiently elaborate stock of colourful words and phrases are they allowed to turn their facts into stories, and then whatever they write must be pruned for public consumption. It would certainly help if someone could do for reporters what Roget, in compiling his thesaurus, did for ordinary writers.

You may have noticed that news stories differ in literary form from most other kinds of writing. The short story, for example, begins at the beginning and proceeds gradually toward a climax, after which it tapers off sharply to a satisfactory conclusion. The news story begins at the end, or at the climax, and proceeds backwards until the reporter runs out of facts or the editor runs out of patience. That's why, in the news, we often learn that people are dead before we know that they were alive.

We can illustrate the difference with a series of incidents in the life of a man, his beloved wife, and their turnip. A short story writer would arrange the series like this:

Jake squirmed nervously in his chair while the judges, score cards in hand, walked solemnly around the hall scribbling notes as they went. This was the day that Jake had been waiting for, but somehow, now that it was here, he didn't at all like it. Something — what was it? — a kind of inner voice, perhaps, told him that the months of toil and near despair had been for nothing. He glanced across the room to where Martha sat — Martha who had stood by him in these trying times, unflinchingly, Martha who even now seemed so much more self-possessed than he, as though fortified by some inner power that he knew nothing of.

Moments before, he had watched her emerge vivaciously from the ladies' luncheon where, although he knew nothing of it, they had served pink gin and sandwiches, and he had been reassured (if reassurance was necessary) that she would stand by him to the end, come what may. The way she seemed to glow from within, the way she tripped so gracefully to her chair, like a ballet dancer, the way she smiled, continuously — everything she did was so typically Martha.

The judges, enigmatic, almost hostile looking, were approaching the platform. Jake glanced again at Martha. He was like a frightened little boy. But Martha, almost oblivious of the tension around her, was a picture of tranquillity and geniality. One of the judges was about to speak. Jake felt a sudden impulse to run away, away from the judges, away from all the people, away from — Martha? No never that. The judge took off his glasses. Jake wiped off his forehead. Martha slipped off her shoes. The people broke off their conversations.

"It is my great pleasure," the judge said, (Jake's heart pounded against his chest as though it would break through. Martha sat imperturbable, the smile still on her face. Gad, she was a woman!) "to announce that the grand champion turnip (This was it. How would he face the defeat he now felt certain would be his? How would Martha face it when there was no longer any doubt? What about the turnips? These were forbidding thoughts.) is the one exhibited by Jake Trapp."

For a moment Jake sat motionless. He could hardly believe his ears. His turnip had won after all. Overpowered by emotion, he made his way toward Martha and, with tears in his eyes, said, "Yippee!" Martha sat smiling, as imperturbable as before. She was asleep.

That's how the short story writers do it. An experienced reporter would do it this way:

TURNIP GROWERS WIFE PASSES OUT
AFTER DRINKING BOUT

Martha Trapp, wife of grand champion turnip grower Jake Trapp, fainted today as the judges announced their decision at the annual Turnip Growers Festival. Although details are lacking, it is believed that while the men were competing with the turnips, the ladies had a competition of their own at the noon luncheon where, it has been authoritatively learned, the main course was pink gin and sandwiches. It has not been determined whether charges will be laid. Mrs. Trapp lost consciousness as her husband was being named grand champion turnip exhibitor by the chairman of the judges' panel. The husband's only comment was "Yippee."

Today's developments were not altogether unexpected, as Mrs. Trapp had been observed earlier trying unsuccessfully to imitate a ballet dancer, grinning at everyone, and kicking off her shoes. Her husband, apparently intent on the deliberations of the judges, seemed not to notice. Although there is nothing official, it is expected that an investigation will be carried out, and pink gin will be removed from the menu of the ladies' luncheon at future festivals.

Not all consumers of news prefer their non-fiction dark. I recall one in particular who accosted me while I was making up headlines. I had just finished typing Three Feared Dead in Plane Crash, when I sensed that he was looking over my shoulder.

"That's the trouble with you people," he said, as I turned to face him. "You're always writing about tragedy."

"It has a way of happening," I said, glancing over the latest edition. The front page screamed death and destruction, a pattern that was repeated, though to a lesser degree, on subsequent pages.

"Three feared dead," he said, reading aloud what I'd typed. "You'll banner that, but you'll not say a word about the hundreds of planes that land safely every day."

"Are there that many?" I asked, for I couldn't remember reading about any.

"And look at this," he said, picking up the newspaper. "Man Assaults Wife. How many times have you printed Man Embraces Wife?"

"Never," I said, blanching under his accusing gaze. It was true. I'd seldom, if ever, read, let alone written, a front page story about a normal or happy husband and wife relationship. In the back pages there had been suggestions: anniversaries, trips abroad together, joint ventures, and the like, but nothing really explicit. Surely there must have been some husbands who didn't beat, desert or kill their wives.

"Historians a thousand years hence," he continued, "with nothing but our newspapers to go by would conclude that we lived in a society of horror, perversion and treachery." He was right. I could see that. We'd been doing this thing wrong for years. Life couldn't be as bad as the papers make it out to be. All cars don't get into accidents, even though most of the ones we read about do. Not every construction worker plunges eighteen storeys to his death. Nor is it really true that whenever someone digs a well a child falls into it.

"You news people traffic in misfortune," the visitor went on in his accusing way. "You deliberately seek it out."

"We do," I confessed, no longer able to look him in the eye. Oh, he was right again. Often I'd seen reporters rush excitedly to their desks to produce tales of agony and mutilation, or wait eagerly at the wire service for word that some statesman or other had died. They weren't waiting to write his obituary. They already had that on file. They just wanted to be there when the word came through.

"It's a question of emphasis," the critic was saying. "You print some good news, but you play it down. It's distortion, that's what it is."

"Yes," I conceded. "We twist things around to make them grotesque." I was beginning to wonder how we had managed to get away with it for so long.

"You've got to think positively," he said. "Write happily. Play up the bright side."

Of course, that was the way to do it. He not only knew what was wrong with the news business. He knew how to set it right.

With that, he left, and I didn't see him again until he'd returned from a trip to New York. He had been chosen a delegate to a stamp collectors convention, a very happy gathering, he said, and would I care to do something about it for the paper. I said I'd be delighted to and the next day we carried the following story:

LOCAL MAN ATTENDS NEW YORK CONVENTION
WITHOUT MISHAP

John Briggs, no known aliases, flew to New York this week to represent local stamp collectors at the annual Philatelists convention. Before take-off, there were no ugly rumours that a bomb had been placed aboard and police did not order the passengers to open their luggage just to be sure. The plane did not crash fifteen minutes out of Toronto, and eighty of the one hundred people aboard were not killed. Nor was it discovered shortly after arrival that the landing gear had been faulty and the fuel supply dangerously low.

The convention took place in one of the city's most respectable hotels, from which no one has been known to jump in a suicide attempt, successful or otherwise. Mr. Briggs received no word during his New York stay of any deaths or misfortunes back home, and happily there was none. Moreover, he himself was not killed, maimed or otherwise inconvenienced while on the trip.

The delegates completed a heavy agenda speedily without bickering or dissension of any sort. Although large quantities of spirits were supplied by generous sponsors, no disorderly conduct was reported. Mr. Briggs did not get disgustingly drunk the final night of the gathering. Nor was he seen with a strange woman reeling down Fifth Avenue at two o'clock the following morning. He was not picked up and fined heavily in a New York court, did not miss his return flight and have to take a later one, and neither the early nor the late plane crashed.

Take Me Out of the Ball Game

I CAN'T GET THE HANG OF BASEBALL. It's much too subtle for me. I know it's enormously popular and the really big players become millionaires part way through the season. But I don't understand it.

I don't understand how people can pay good money to watch other people watch. Baseball is mainly about watching. The paying customers watch the players and the players spend most of their time watching each other. Some of them lounge around and watch from the dugout. Others stand around and watch from the field.

I know what they're watching, but I don't understand why. I don't see how all those customers and athletes can waste a Wednesday evening or a Saturday afternoon watching two people trying to play catch while a third tries to stop them. I'm sure there must be more to it than that, but I can't see it. Perhaps if I'd been born in the United States, where baseball came to maturity, I'd be able to see it. But I wasn't and I can't.

The main activity seems to be chewing, spitting, hitching up pants and scratching. They're very good at it, which probably explains the high salaries. Little else happens unless the batter — he's the one trying to stop the game of catch — manages to hit the ball. As soon as he makes contact, he gallops out of there as fast as he can. Whoever gets the ball throws it at him, but seldom scores a direct hit. Then they start playing catch again and another player tries to break it up.

I've had it explained to me several times. I've been told about strikes and balls, base hits and home runs. It sounds like fun except for the waiting and watching in between. I get bored waiting and I fall asleep watching. I imagine the players would, too, if it weren't for the chewing, spitting, hitching and scratching. All that activity keeps them alert in case something happens.

One of the worst things that can happen is a foul ball. A ball goes foul when the batter hits it out of play. When it comes back in, from who knows where, the umpire is understandably concerned, and handles it gingerly. So is the pitcher, who tries to clean it up before throwing it to the catcher. Just by the look on his face you can tell how foul it is.

Some of the players are openly religious. They sign themselves, look up to the heavens and pray aloud when something goes wrong. Often in the dugout they meditate privately. Sometimes the manager walks out on the field and meets the catcher and pitcher for a brief prayer on the mound. Occasionally, he and the umpire face each other in Gregorian chant. Sometimes the spectators rise up en masse and speak in tongues.

As you will have gathered, baseball is not really a team sport. It's more like a series of one-on-ones. If hockey and basketball were like baseball, they'd consist of one penalty — or free — shot after another. In baseball, it's one at bat after another. Oh, I know it's supposed to get exciting when there's one or more players on base, but all the waiting and watching until that happens is tedious.

I'd rather watch the popcorn venders. They're more active than the players.

If it weren't for television, I'd have given up baseball long ago. I don't watch the games live. I record them for later viewing. Then I can fast forward all the waiting, watching, chewing, spitting, hitching, scratching, foul-ball sniffing, and praying. That leaves just the hits and runs, which is what baseball is about. Isn't it?

How Jazz Began

FOR MORE THAN a quarter century, I've played trumpet in a locally tolerated dixieland band. It's only a sideline, of course. It's not something I could ever make a living out of. It's just a challenging hobby. The local music reviewers understand this. They've often complimented me for being musically challenged.

One of them even said I reminded him of the great jazz trumpeter Bobby Hackett, who is now, unfortunately, dead. I was genuinely touched. I would have preferred being compared to the live Bobby Hackett, but I wouldn't think of making an issue of it. Apart from his superior tone, technique, style and creativity, Hackett and I had a great deal in common. He always worked with three valves as I do, and I normally direct the sound out of the bell of my horn as he invariably did.

But some reviewers can be downright nasty with our group. They think nothing of scolding us about our age and drinking habits. One of them, a local doctor who fancies himself a jazz buff, has accused us of groping our collective way to the bandstand. If Dr. Buff had any musical judgment, he would realize that groping is not what we do on the way to the bandstand. Groping is what happens after we reach the bandstand. We have trouble finding the notes. That's why we haven't introduced any new tunes in the last decade. We'd like to learn the old ones first.

And that's not booze people see us with. We don't drink on the stand. We do take non-steroidal anti-inflammatory drugs, insulin and several varieties of phenothiazines. If we didn't, one third of us would stiffen up like Frankenstein's monster, one sixth would go into a coma, and the rest would go mad. When Dr. Buff takes notes while we're playing, he's not just reviewing the music. He's making clinical observations.

Another reviewer has accused us of plagiarism because we quote excerpts of copyrighted songs in our ad-lib solos without obtaining permission from the publishers. We would never consciously do such a thing. Unconsciously, perhaps. You see, when you've been around as long as we have, your attention span shortens and it's easy to lose your train of thought. So if you're taking a chorus on "I've Found a New Baby", you might absentmindedly wander into "Baby Face". Or, if you're playing "Rockin' Chair", you might take a side trip through "Don't Get Around Much Anymore". None of which explains the musical and anatomical connection between "Black Bottom" and "Cheek to Cheek".

But it's all very innocent and unintentional, like trying to play a flatted fifth and, instead, producing a strangled seventh, or reaching for an augmented fourth and ending up with a diminished capacity.

Only the most dedicated aficionados would be interested in the complex theory underlying all of this. Few music lovers concern themselves with crescendos, diminuendos, libidos and pink flamingos. Fewer still care about adagio, andante, on Donder and Blitzen. Classical musicians have chided us about our allegretto. We'd just as soon have pepperoni and play incognito.

It's not the reviewers' fault that they don't know what we're about. Misinformation has plagued jazz from its inception in New Orleans nearly a century ago. The histories tell you that it was invented by musicians like Buddy Bolden and Bunk Johnson. The histories are wrong. Jazz originated from defective musical instruments and indigestion.

The people who first played it couldn't be sure when they blew their hand-me-down cornets, clarinets and trombones that the instruments would respond. More often than not, they responded a quarter of a beat late. The result was syncopation, a key element in jazz. Creole cooking did the rest, as anyone who has overindulged in this southern delight might readily appreciate. As they alternated desperately between striving to produce the notes and straining to suppress the hiccups, the pioneers of jazz established the rhythmic counterpoint that later became known as swing.

Of course they were too preoccupied to realize that they were giving birth to a new musical genre. Listeners noticed, however, and greeted their efforts with enthusiastic cries of "It's a gas." Nothing like this happened with the more affluent uptown musicians. Their instruments were in excellent working order and they could afford bicarbonate of soda. Consequently, they were doomed to play tunes like "The Carnival of Venice", and play them straight.

Bebop, also known as progressive jazz, arrived in the 1940s. It began with musicians like Dizzy Gillespie, who converted to Islam and changed their diets as a result. This sparked a whole new class of gastrointestinal disturbances that erupted in incredible technical flourishes and an epidemic of flatted fifths. Students of language were quick to authenticate the change by pointing out that flatted has the same linguistic root as flatulent.

Popular music shifted radically in the 1950s and '60s with the advent of rock 'n' roll. Unlike jazz, which swings, rock jerks and twitches. More neurological than gastrointestinal, these musical convulsions are attributed to the wide array of chemical additives food processors introduced at the time. Only the relatively few jazz artists who insisted on natural fare escaped the rhythmic mutation. The rest, to varying degrees, fell into a hybrid style which some authorities call jazz-rock fusion. Others call it *con*fusion.

No one knows when we will see another jazz breakthrough, but I rather suspect it will take place at an international food fair. These multicultural extravaganzas offer enough exotic treats to fuel a musical revolution. I don't expect our band will be a part of it, though. Our instruments work and we're too old to change our eating habits.

For Him the Bell Tolled

LITERARY SCHOLARS have authenticated a lost manuscript by one of the leading writers of the twentieth century. The discovery reveals exciting new details about the travels on which the famous author based some of his best work. More important, it shows that adventure writers need not seek out exotic places for material and inspiration. The following is an excerpt from what is being hailed as a historic literary find.

SASKATCHEWAN SAFARI

by

Hemest Erningway

Lying in the deep grass as the sun started up, the dew seeping through our jackets, the fresh green smell rising, we saw the big cat at the edge of a bluff below, slowly stalking the cattle that stood like sculptures in the flat pasture.

"That's the one," I said, getting the cougar in my sights.

"That's got to be the one," Charlie said.

"It's the one, all right," I said. " I've never seen a mountain lion that big."

"He's a monster and he's ready to jump," Charlie said. I heard him take the safety off.

He was certainly a big cat, at least ten feet from his black-tipped tail to his nose and weighing more than a hundred and fifty pounds. Through the grass and trees, I could see his tawny-coloured coat with the buff below and his small head and focused face. Then he made his move toward a sagging cow at the edge of the herd.

"I've got him," Charlie said and fired. A flock of prairie chicken exploded from a wheat field beside the pasture and all but one of the cattle stampeded to the fence on the far side. The one that stayed behind lay like a lump of earth on the short cropped pasture. The cougar was nowhere to be seen.

"You got the cow, Charlie," I said. "You got him good."

"Didn't I, though?"

"That's one cow that thievin' cat won't get to kill."

"I got her just in time, all right."

"You sure did, Charlie. You got her just in time. What's more, you scared the hell out of that big cougar."

"That cougar won't be coming around here for a while, I can tell you."

"Let's go after him, anyhow," I said, getting up from the damp grass, my legs stiff with the early morning chill.

"Yeah, let's finish him off," Charlie said.

We had been hired by a group of farmers to do something about a huge cougar that was feasting on cattle along the banks of the Saskatchewan River, where deep brush and thick clumps of stunted trees provided cover. The big cat had reached almost mythic proportions in the minds of the farmers who hired us. They acted as if there was something supernatural about him and they wanted him out of there.

We hurried past where the dead cow lay, a large hole about where her lungs were and blood pooled by her open mouth and snout, to the edge of the bluff the cougar had leapt out from. Charlie bent down to study the big cat's tracks.

"That way," he said, pointing toward the river, as it curved around a large outcropping of rock and flowed northeastward toward Saskatoon.

"I think he went that way, all right," I said.

"If he didn't go that way, he's walking backwards," Charlie said.

After going a short distance, I saw a pile of fresh cougar dung, the stink rising and causing us to cover our faces.

"I sure scared him good," Charlie said

"You scared him good, all right, Charlie," I said. "He won't be coming around here for a while."

"He sure won't be coming around here," Charlie agreed.

We walked along for a while without saying anything. At length, Charlie stopped and shook his head.

"That cougar dung sure stinks," he said.

"Yeah, it stinks, all right, Charlie."

"I can still smell it."

"You stepped in it, Charlie."

We tracked the cougar to a narrow road that headed on toward the highway that led into town. Charlie bent down and inspected the surface of the road and the dust on top that shifted with the rising breeze.

"It's a hard call," Charlie said. "Either he crossed this road, or he didn't."

"That's probably true, Charlie," I said. I wondered whether cougars made choices the way we did. Charlie was considering the same thing.

"Those big dumb cats think like we do," Charlie said. "They weigh the evidence and then decide. I think he decided to go down the road a stretch and then double back the way he came to throw us off the scent. Let's go across the road to that bluff and wait him out."

We went across and hunkered down in the bluff, the rising breeze fluttering the leaves and lifting the dust off the road like smoke. We could hear a big grain truck coming down the road, tearing apart the early morning silence. Just then we caught sight of the cougar on the edge of the low bushes along the other side of the road. We knew we had to act before the truck spooked the big cat and we both got off a couple of rounds in record time. There was a deafening crash and the earth seemed to shake beneath us.

"We got the grain truck, Charlie," I said.

"We sure as hell did," Charlie said.

We got up and went over to where the truck had left the road and knocked over a big poplar tree. There were a couple of bullet holes in the side of the truck and the farmer who had been driving it was climbing out, all shaken up and babbling nonsense.

"Would you look at that," Charlie said, pointing to the front of the truck where the big cougar was pinned under the wheels, his neck broken and his legs spread out like a polar bear rug.

"That was some shooting, Charlie," I said.

"That sure was some shooting," Charlie said. "We knocked the truck off the road and into that big cougar just fine."

The farmer was beginning to make sense and came around to have a look at the cougar.

"So that's the cat who's been causing all the trouble," he said.

"That's him," said Charlie. "Give us a hand, will you, to get off his tail. We need it to collect our bounty."

The War of the Words

IT'S NOT PRETTY what's going on in the English language. Words are fighting it out for verbal supremacy and the carnage is devastating. Look what's happening to the verb *affect*. It's being ruthlessly supplanted by the noun *impact*. We used to feel comfortable saying things like "Good health affects everything." Now, we feel pressured into saying "Good health impacts everything." I don't know how *impact* gets away with masquerading as a verb and conning journalists, politicians, bureaucrats, jurists, clergy and just about everyone else into yielding to its grammatical pretensions. *Impact* is not alone, of course. All kinds of words are deceitfully shifting from one part of speech to another, trying to gain a syntactical advantage.

I guess I can understand why a frumpy noun like *impact* would want to transform itself into a verb. Verbs are where the action is. They're the grammatical movers and shakers. For the life of me, I can't understand why a dapper verb like *read* would want to transform itself into a noun. But this is exactly what that silly verb is doing. In the imperative sentence "Read *Hamlet*!" it projects an inescapable air of power and self-assurance. In the indicative sentence "*Hamlet* is a good read" it comes off as a wimp.

Saw and *seen* are in a life and death struggle that is inflicting heavy casualties on the auxiliary verbs *has*, *have* and *had*. We used to easily form sentences like "We saw that show three years ago and we have seen it a couple of times since." That was before *seen* gained the momentum. Now, many of us are just as likely to say "We seen that show three years ago and we seen it a couple of times since." It's the worst case of verbal cleansing since *can* supplanted *may* in sentences like "Can I please leave the room?"

The personal pronouns *I* and *me* have been battling fiercely for years and in some sectors *me* appears to be winning. What's more, it doesn't have to transform itself into another part of speech to carry the day. It merely has to undergo a change of case, from object to subject. Hence, particularly among the young, we hear sentences like "Me and Horace are going to the show. Can me and the guys have something to eat? If there was any justice, me and you would be rich." I really feel for *I*, which has only one letter to *me*'s two. I wish *me* would pick on a word its own size.

Less, a seemingly insignificant adjective, is one of the most aggressive words in the language. It has all but eliminated *fewer* from polite conversation. I can remember when *less* was content to denote things collectively as in the sentence "He has less money than he used to." Not anymore. Now, *less* insists on denoting things individually as well, a task that *fewer* used to perform with distinction, as in the sentence "He has fewer dollars than he used to." Once *less* went into action, poor old *fewer* didn't stand a chance and it's a rare print, radio or TV news story that doesn't contain sentences like "Less spectators attended than were expected. Summer jobs attracted less applicants this year than last. Blaming failing eyesight, the once proud birder spotted less Baltimore orioles than he usually does."

It's puzzling why so many words are dissatisfied with their station in life. To try to find out, I decided to interview *less*.

"*Less*," I said, "why are you so cruelly ousting *fewer* from the language? *Fewer* never harmed anyone as far as I can see and was doing a good job."

"It's a word-eat-word world out there," *less* replied. "I'm in the comparative business and if I'm going to get ahead, I've got to beat the competition."

"But if every word did that we'd be in a grammatical nightmare."

"If that's what you're worried about, you should be talking to *more*. *More* has had a syntactical advantage over me from the beginning and it's not fair."

With that, he brought the interview to an abrupt end, stomping off to denote a new batch of nouns individually. From what he said about *more*, I suspected that his ruthlessness was fuelled by envy. Not only does *more* denote things individually, as in "More beans, please," it denotes them collectively, as in "More food, please." The grammarians appear to be treating *more* preferentially and *less* has reached the point where he's no longer going to put up with it. That's why he's undergoing a syntax change.

I'm not especially worried about the dominance of words like *closure*, *awesome* and *cool*. Oh, I know that just about everyone is looking for closure on one thing or another, that most new experiences are awesome, and that all sorts of trendy people and popular pursuits are cool. But all-purpose words like these wear themselves out rather quickly and give way to others just as imprecise. That didn't stop me from trying to find out what motivates them. I failed, however. Those clichés are so full of themselves they don't grant interviews to the likes of me.

Bewitched by Birders

I BECAME INTERESTED in bird watching through a misunderstanding. I had just finished seeing the Toronto Blue Jays on television, when my next-door neighbour came over.

"There's a Baltimore oriole outside," he said breathlessly.

"Save it for April Fool's day, will you, Charlie."

"No, I'm serious. There's a Baltimore oriole in the backyard."

"Which one?"

"Yours."

"Mine?"

"Yeah, your backyard."

"I mean which Baltimore Oriole?"

"Does it really matter? Come on and see for yourself."

I grabbed my autograph book and followed him out to the back. I thought it might be some kind of personal appearance. Maybe it had something to do with the contests I get inveigled into entering from time to time.

"Well?" I said, when we stood alone together on the patio.

"Here, take the binoculars." He pointed to the willow that dominated my backyard. I adjusted the focus and inspected the tree.

"All I can see is a bird," I said.

"Yeah, a Baltimore oriole."

"You mean to say they named a bird after a baseball team?"

That was my introduction to bird watching. Until then, I scarcely knew that bird watchers existed. Now, I seldom miss an opportunity to see them in action. I could watch bird watchers all day. Birds are another story. After a while, I lose interest in birds. I never lose interest in birders.

Birder, by the way, is an officially recognized label, like fisher. It's interesting, though, that whereas a birder is a bird watcher a fisher is not a fish watcher. A fisher is a fish catcher. The last thing a birder wants to do is catch a bird. He just wants to look at it, identify it, count it and boast about it.

Birders number into the millions and birding is so popular it's becoming respectable. I suspect that people who want to look at wildlife undisturbed will soon have to resort to insect watching. Bugs are even more numerous and varied than birds. But if a bird watcher is a birder, what will we call a bug watcher? I thought so, too.

It's amazing how much you can learn hanging out with birders. I used to think that most birds just whistled. Well, they're much more versatile than that. They can peep, warble, screech, squawk, hiss, croak, cackle and hoot and the more vain ones, like the chickadee and the killdeer, call their own names, over and over again. When the male Canada goose says "a-honk", the female replies "hink" and then they alternate a-honk, hink, a-honk, hink through the entire relationship. Canada geese mate for life. With a vocabulary like that, no one else will have them.

Birders have marvelous memories. The way they can recite the names of one species of bird after another fascinates me. I don't know how they do it. I certainly can't do it. It's all I can do to recite the names of one species of bird watcher after another. Not only do birders give you the common names of the different species — if you're not careful, they'll add the scientific names. I'll bet you didn't know that the scientific name for Baltimore oriole is *Icterus galbula*. Neither did I until my neighbour caught me off guard and jumped at the chance to show off his Latin. I'm just thankful he didn't tell me the scientific name for blue jay. It's bad enough watching my favourite team lose in English.

Birders are remarkably observant. What they don't see, they hear, and what they don't hear, they suspect. One summer morning I was with a group of them when they announced in unison, "yellow-bellied sapsucker on the left." As usual, I missed it. While they were watching the yellow-bellied sapsucker on the left, I couldn't help noticing the ruby-beaked rye sipper on the right. The ruby-beaked rye sipper is a bird watcher whose fake binoculars hold enough whisky to enable him to see anything you care to suggest. A solitary performer, he waits until his companions are otherwise engaged before putting the field glasses to his lips.

On the same trip, the group crept off to try to authenticate a MacGillivray's warbler, no doubt named after the ornithologist who first described the species. As luck would have it, I was left staring at an O'Brien's peeping tom, named after the policeman who first arrested one. The O'Brien's peeping tom is a committed bird watcher. He differs from other species in that he prefers training his binoculars on birds that perch in front of bedroom windows.

On different outings I've learned to distinguish the red-breasted nuthatch, the fork-tailed flycatcher and the ring-necked pheasant, all birds, from the bare-chested nutcase, the fork-tongued chatter box and the red-necked peasant, all birders. The bare-chested nutcase is noted for strutting around in the semi-nude, preening himself on his physique. The fork-tongued chatter box claims to see birds that no one else does and never stops talking about them. The red-necked peasant refuses to watch birds of colour.

I also know the difference between the western bluebird and the prairie bluebeard. The prairie bluebeard is more interested in watching female birders than male or female birds. Unlike most birders, he tries to capture the objects of his affection and run off with them. The prairie bluebeard is a birder of prey. But he's no match for the sharp-tongued grouser, who complains loud and long at the slightest hint of harassment, or the catty birder, a vicious tattler.

Some birders are unrepentant name droppers. At every opportunity they mention the names of rare birds they want you to think they've identified and listed. They don't fool me, though. I can tell when they haven't done their field work. I can see that all the name dropping is just a bid for status. Whether from birders or birds, there's nothing impressive about droppings.

Song birders are among the easiest to identify. Some of them try to mimic the music of the birds they're searching for. This irritates their companions, who prefer the genuine article. Others try to get into the spirit of the search by humming or singing bits and pieces of once popular songs dedicated to birds: "Snowbird", "Skylark", "Bye Bye Blackbird", things like that. This irritates the birds, who feel exploited because they derive no royalties from the songs.

There are places where you don't have to go looking for birds. They come looking for you. St. Mark's Square in Venice is one of my favourites. If rock doves are your passion, St. Mark's is the place for you. The rock dove, of course, is the common domestic pigeon, whose chief identifying feature is defaced public monuments. In St. Mark's, there are so many pigeons they fly in shifts. It's no trick to watch them. The trick is to watch out for them. Fortunately, there are churches nearby to seek refuge in. We call them birder sanctuaries.

Father's Little Helpers

MY GOOD NEIGHBOUR Farnsworth prides himself on being a passable husband and father. I believe his pride is largely justified. So, I suspect, do Mrs. Farnsworth and their teenage daughters, Susan and Corinne. All three are adequately attentive, tolerably respectful and rarely abusive. You might say that Farnsworth has reached that stage in life where he is decently happy, having come to terms with marriage and learned to accept parenthood.

The day before Father's Day, his daughters announced that they were going to take him downtown and buy him a new necktie.

"How delightful," Farnsworth said, wincing. Though he appreciated the thought, he was not much of a shopper and ties were the article of clothing he favoured least.

"I rarely wear the ones I've got," he protested mildly.

"That's why you need a new one," they chirped.

"Besides," Susan said, "we want to observe your special day."

"Yes," said Corinne, "we've been saving up for it."

"Well, this is really very kind of you," he said, capitulating.

Declaring it a wonderful idea, his wife decided to go along for the ride and allow Farnsworth to buy them lunch.

On the way to the ties, they strolled through the women's clothing department.

"Isn't that divine?" Susan said, pointing to a plaid jacket. "Wait while I try it on."

A half hour and several jackets later, she selected what she thought was the most suitable, but her sister wasn't sure. While they discussed their differences, Farnsworth glanced absentmindedly at his watch and suppressed a yawn.

"I wish you wouldn't do that, Dear," his wife said. "Go over to the book department and read."

Happily, he left them. Another half hour went by before they came for him.

"We're famished. Let's eat," the girls said.

"What about the jacket?" he asked, reluctantly putting down the book he had been looking into.

"We've settled on one," Mrs. Farnsworth said, "but she'll need a new skirt for it. We'll have to go back after we've eaten."

Over lunch, the women discussed Farnsworth's ties and how he really ought to upgrade the lot of them. Susan said he looked ever so much better in a tie than in an open collar. Corinne suggested that ties were making a spectacular comeback in men's fashions. Farnsworth listened respectfully, though skeptically.

"This is going to be the best Father's Day ever," the girls trilled in unison as he paid the bill.

"We won't be a minute, Dear," Mrs. Farnsworth said when they arrived in women's clothing. "Go back to the book department and read."

He became so absorbed in his book he lost track of time. When Mrs. Farnsworth interrupted him, he seemed surprised to see her.

"Is anything wrong?" he said

"Not really," his wife replied. "We've got Susan taken care of, but we're having difficulty fitting Corinne. She needs a new blouse and a pair of shoes. Why don't you take us for coffee?"

He did, after which Mrs. Farnsworth sent him back to the book department to read, while she and the girls waded yet again into women's clothing. It was the girls who interrupted him next. Radiating happiness, they told him their purchases were complete but they weren't quite ready to leave, as Mrs. Farnsworth was trying on hats.

"Mom sent us for your credit card," Corinne said.

He surrendered it.

"You stay right here, Father, and read," Susan said. "We'll be back in no time." They hurried off.

Lost in his book, he failed to respond to the voices that contended with the story line for his attention. Only a tug on the sleeve broke his concentration.

"Really, Dear," Mrs. Farnsworth said, "you must get your nose out of that book and come along. We've got to be home soon to start making supper."

Loaded down with parcels and bags, he followed them to the men's department, where ties in all colours and designs hung or lay about like mini-tapestries.

"That one will do," he said, nodding to the narrowest and least conspicuous specimen he could see.

The women were aghast.

"You're not getting off that easy," Susan said.

"You've got to pick a special tie for a special day," said Corinne.

"Show some imagination, Dear," Mrs. Farnsworth urged.

Try as he may, he couldn't find anything that satisfied all three of them. Two out of three was the best he could do.

"I'm afraid you've left it too late," Mrs. Farnsworth said, scolding him gently. "The girls will have to try again next Father's Day."

With that, the women allowed him to carry what they had bought to the car and chauffeur them home.

On Father's Day, they were especially attentive to Farnsworth, modelling their purchases for his enjoyment and detailing how much they had saved by getting everything on sale. They were so pleased with themselves they thought it would be a splendid gesture if Farnsworth took them to dinner to celebrate his special day. They said he could pay for it out of the money they had saved him.

"You deserve it, Dear," Mrs. Farnsworth said, and she told him to go into the study and read while she made the reservation.

The Main Event

WHEN I LAST WENT SOUTH for a little sun, some friends took me to a magnificent arena. It featured a powerful sound system playing the hits of a celebrated group I wasn't familiar with. I think it was called Human Remains. Could that band pump out the decibels! It was like listening to a series of explosions.

There were TV sets mounted below the circular ceiling so that no matter where you sat you could see one or two of them and watch commercials and other visuals, and in the centre was a huge clock with an enormous display area. The clock showed commercials, cartoons and logos; and from time to time giant sub-titles and excited voices exhorted us to applaud, cheer or just make noise and more noise. Radio controlled dirigibles that looked like cola bottles, automobiles and animals floated around and occasionally released coupons that could be exchanged for merchandize.

On every level, the halls outside the amphitheatre had rows of fast food and drink outlets. People were continually going out and coming back in with popcorn, potato chips, hot dogs, burgers, chocolate bars, ice cream cones and huge plastic glasses full of soft drinks or beer. Periodically, vendors with trays of food appeared at the exits and bellowed.

There was also a hockey game going on.

But that didn't bother anyone. No matter what happened on the ice, the fans beat time to the band, responded on cue to the clock, snatched coupons out of the air and repeatedly went out to replenish their food and drink supply. Oh, there were some who seemed annoyed when the referee dropped the puck for a face-off and the music cut out while the teams played. But these whiners didn't have much to complain about because as soon as the whistle blew to stop the action the band blasted away again and everyone could go back to rockin' and rollin'.

It was my first National Hockey League game since the NHL consisted of six teams. Now it consists of a hundred and six, or so it seems. I've watched lots of NHL games on TV. But that's not the same as being there. Except for the commercials, all you get on TV is the game and the play-by-play account. In the arena, you get the big picture. Why, in some seats you can practically reach out and touch the food vendors.

Hockey was once a winter sport. Now, it goes on year round. Hockey players used to come from the North and hockey teams were domiciled in northern cities. Now, the players come from anywhere and the teams can be located in the tropics. All of this is due to the development and expansion of artificial ice. When I first saw it, I didn't know the difference between artificial and natural ice. I know now. When water freezes naturally, it expands, but not much. When it freezes artificially, it expands all over and hockey expands with it.

Artificial ice is also responsible for the huge increase in the number of women who play hockey at most levels. That's because artificial ice has turned hockey into an indoor sport. When I was growing up, hockey players honed their skills outside. Some never got to play on artificial ice. Now, some never get to play on natural ice.

Women's teams are showing that it's possible to play hockey without fighting. Male hockey players like to fight. Female hockey players would rather talk. You're not likely to see a bench-clearing brawl in a women's hockey game. You might see a bench-clearing conversation.

Some foresee the day when women's and men's teams will be allowed to play against each other. I don't think it will happen, certainly not at the upper levels. If the men won, the women would talk them out of it.

Like every Canadian boy, I wanted to make the NHL. Although I had no aptitude for hockey, I played my heart out anyhow. It was the thing to do. I couldn't afford new skates or much equipment. I bought my first pair of skates second hand and traded them in every year for a larger pair. By the time my feet stopped growing, my ineptitude could no longer be denied and I quit playing. It's a good thing, too, because all I had for protection were second-hand shin pads, regulation gloves and pants and, oh yes, a hockey stick. I wasn't much good at using the stick to protect the net, but I was pretty good at using it to protect myself.

Nowadays, kids start playing hockey at increasingly younger ages. Some learn to skate before they can walk. The sport is so organized and regulated it makes school seem like a holiday The kids can't wait to get back to class for rest and recreation. They can take their frustrations out on the teachers without penalty, but not on the coaches or the referees.

You wouldn't believe the armour these youngsters get into to play a friendly game of hockey. With their helmets, cages, visors, face masks, and padding for shoulders, elbows, shins and other sensitive parts, they look like aliens from another planet.

All of this gear is necessary to protect them from angry parents. In my day, we didn't need it. When we played outdoors, few parents showed up because of the cold. Now that the games are indoors, parents turn out in force, and they're prepared to use force on behalf of their gladiators. Victory has become a matter of parental pride, a berth in the NHL, an object of parental ambition. The officials are pretty good at controlling abuse from players, but not from parents.

I guess some parents are mesmerized by the big money the NHL pays hockey players. The really good ones make millions, and that's just for signing up. For playing, they earn enough in a year to retire from hockey for life. Some of them do, and they have to be traded to another team. I'm sure you'll agree that it's pretty good pay for playing backup to rock 'n' roll, animated commercials, faceless cheerleaders, coupon-dispensing blimps, non-stop booze and chow, and pop-up vendors.

All You Can Eat

I'M NOT A FUSSY EATER. I'm an adventurous eater, in fact. I'm especially adventurous with exotic fare. When invited to dine with friends of different ethnic backgrounds, I eat everything they offer, and drink everything in sight. The hardest thing about eating foreign foods is getting the names straight and pronouncing them right, but that rarely holds me back.

I'm not as adventurous as some orientals, though. The Japanese are great seafood eaters. They even eat fish raw. They call it sushi. Although I'm a great land food eater, I won't eat beef or poultry raw, no matter what they call it. Some connoisseurs prefer their oysters live. I can't bring myself to bite into a live chicken. It might bite back. As long as they're dead and cooked, I can eat fish, poultry, swine and cattle in just about any arrangement. I especially like fish paddies. I like them even better than cow pies.

One dish you won't catch me eating is poached salmon. Poaching is against the law. So if I happen to eat some, you won't catch me at it. I'm adventurous; I'm not reckless. You won't catch me eating bird's nest soup, either. Oh, I know it's a dish the Chinese pride themselves on, but I don't much care for it, anymore than I'd care for hen house salad, pig pen stew or rabbit hole pudding. The Chinese also pride themselves on won ton soup. I like that a lot. Although not as spicy, it's much safer to eat than their hot and bothered soup.

Chicken, I suspect, is the most multicultural of the edible meats. Thanks to recipes from abroad, teriyaki chicken, satay chicken, chicken egg foo yong, chicken souvlaki and chicken frajolaki are among the exotic poultry dishes that edify our pallets and terrify our fowl. So are chicken cordon bleu, chicken cacciatore, chicken carcinoma and chicken carborundum. When I was growing up, all we did with chicken was roast it, pan fry it or boil it. Now, we've acquired a taste for honey and garlic barbecued chicken wings and deep-fried chicken fingers. Until recently, I didn't know chickens had fingers. We've also grown fond of sweet and sour chicken balls. I didn't know that either.

I can't resist Vietnamese ginger chicken. In fact, I'm partial to just about every dish the Vietnamese offer. I like their music, too. I especially like Vietnamese waltzes. My favourite is "Tales from the Vietnam Woods." Perhaps you've heard it.

Curried chicken is a specialty of the East Indians. They also enjoy curried shrimp, curried black beans, curried chickpeas, curried quack grass — curried anything, I suspect. Some North American Indians used to enjoy coureurs de bois, which are now unfortunately extinct. I guess the aboriginals ate too many of them.

Several foods lend themselves to being stuffed. My favourite is stuffed green peppers. Other aficionados prefer stuffed grape leaves, stuffed eggplant, stuffed zucchini, or stuffed Zamboni. No meal is complete without a salad. A plain old lettuce salad is hard to beat if the lettuce is crisp, a spinach salad is tasty when the spinach is fresh, a crab salad is appetizing as long as the crab is tender, a chef salad is delectable provided the chef is not too tough.

Mexican food rarely disappoints me. I love casitas, fajitas, margaritas and senoritas, though not necessarily in that order. I also like refried beans and other leftovers. As for Italian food, I can take it or leave it. Ravioli, fettucini, linguini, and Houdini don't do much for me. Neither do spaghetti or confetti, or for that matter pasta and its nemesis antipasto.

Though not a vegetarian, I enjoy most meatless meals. There's not a bean I can't eat and beans are big with vegetarians. Even small beans are big with vegetarians. They eat green beans, yellow beans, purple beans, broad beans, narrow beans, kidney beans, garbanzo beans, pinto beans, lima beans and especially soybeans. What's great about soybeans is that they can look, feel and taste like just about any meat dish. The other day I sampled a soybean treat that resembled a pork pie. It had the taste, the texture, the appearance, the food value — in fact, everything a pig could produce but the oink. A simulated chicken burger had everything but the cluck.

I realize I've touched on an animal rights issue. As we substitute lentils for livestock, we exclude and marginalize pigs and chickens, not to mention cattle and sheep. If vegetarianism takes over, they'll no longer find a place in our diets and will have to fend for themselves. This, no doubt, is why I feel guilty whenever I go into a restaurant and thoughtlessly choose pasta over pepper steak or hummus over ham. No wonder increasing numbers of farm animals show up as road kill. They're trying to get our attention. It's their way of protesting against blatant discrimination. As a gesture of solidarity, I've a good mind to swear off yogurt, tofu, kung foo, snafu and all the rest of it.

If it weren't for herbs and spices, vegetarian fare would be too bland to enjoy and vegetarians would return to more equitable diets and leave the rest of us alone. The spice I like best is cayenne pepper. I keep a jar of it to perk up my stir fries and a spray can of it to ward of aggressive meat haters.

A Patient's Lament

Since doctors come in two flavours, male and female, the following is mostly written in what progressive grammarians call the plural inclusive.

THE MEDICAL RECORD is mixed.

On the one hand, they keep discovering new ways of treating old diseases. That's clever. I hope they continue. On the other hand, they keep discovering new diseases. That's stupid. Why don't they just stop looking?

Louis Pasteur discovered how to kill germs by getting surgeons to wash their hands and sterilize their instruments. But all that bother would have been unnecessary if he hadn't discovered the germs in the first place. It sounds like a make-work project to me.

A doctor named Alois Alzheimer was so excited when he discovered a devastating form of dementia that he named it after himself. That's fine for him, but what about the patients who have to live with it? At least the doctor who discovered amyotrophic lateral sclerosis had the humility to credit Lou Gehrig, the baseball star who died of it.

When you're my age, you can't help wondering what's going to cause your own death. I hope it's something straightforward like prostate cancer or cardiac arrest. I don't want it to be something exotic like Hansen's disease or Kaposi's sarcoma. I mean what did Hansen or Kaposi have against me?

If I developed a new drug or vaccine, I'd be proud to give my name to it. That's what Jonas Salk did and we bless him every time we think about poliomyelitis. If I discovered a new disease, I wouldn't tell a soul about it, let alone give it my name. Why would I want people I don't even know to curse me?

And yet, medical scientists scour the earth in pursuit of disease, and when they find something new, they argue about who saw it first. What's scary for us patients is that if they fail to discover something new, they're liable to rediscover something old. Just when I thought tuberculosis was extinct, it's become fashionable again, and in some places where they said they'd got rid of malaria, it's as popular as ever. The other day when I asked our medical health officer about smallpox, I could swear I saw a twinkle in his eye.

Thank goodness most doctors aren't researchers. They're not interested in what's wrong with the world. They're interested in what's wrong with us. Diagnosis, in fact, is a major part of what they do. But to excel at it, they need cases that challenge them. We patients can help by keeping them guessing.

If they ask, "How are you?" the proper response is. "You tell me. Isn't that what we pay you for?" If they inquire about specific complaints, the standard reply should be, "Come on, Doc, that's cheating. Use your technology, read your medical books, consult your colleagues."

Remember, you have the right to remain silent. Anything you say may be held against you in the court of medical opinion. Remember, too, that not just what you say but how you act can give you away. So watch your body language.

This may seem unco-operative and rude, but it isn't. By parrying their questions, or remaining silent, we keep them sharp and get to see how good they are. Besides, we wouldn't want to say or do anything that could mislead them.

By all means allow them to inspect your tongue, examine your eyes, peer into your ears and pull your hair. Let them tap your bones to see if they're hollow, listen to your heart to see if its beating, press your stomach to see if it's digesting, probe your bowels to see if they're moving. Permit them to explore your nether regions with practised fingers and blunt instruments, the blunter the better. Don't object if they want to sample your blood, and if they ask for urine, give generously.

Sometimes they'll send you out for more exotic tests. Take all you can get. Don't worry if they want you to have your brain scanned, your spine tapped, your bones scraped, your stomach pumped. It's all part of the diagnosis. And for goodness sake don't let them intimidate you with those big words they use. They're just trying to impress you. If they keep it up, impress them right back. Tell them you've got a friend with a rare form of the kissing disease, supercalifragilisticmononucleosis.

As a last resort, they may refer you to a specialist. By all means, go. But be careful. Specialists are more persistent than general practitioners and more likely to find something wrong with you.

We usually survive medical check-ups with few lasting ill effects. But nobody lives forever. If we insist on regular visits, our doctors will eventually have bad news for us, an inoperable tumor, an incurable infection, a terminal impotency. Addressing this requires delicacy and sensitivity. If they avoid eye contact, ask them to sit down. If they seem distressed, suggest something to relax them. If they appear short of breath, be ready to call 911. Above all stay calm and avoid saying anything that might upset them. We need our doctors.

The Theory of Devolution

THE THEORY OF EVOLUTION has never made sense to me. The evidence is all the other way. It doesn't suggest that we evolved from lower life forms at all. It suggests that lower life forms are devolving from us. You just have to look at the historic and prehistoric records to see what I mean. Both tell us that we've been in persistent decline from the beginning.

One of the few things we know for certain about our distant past is that in prehistoric times we wore animal skins. What this indicates is that our ability to withstand the elements, as other mammals do, was already diminishing. To compensate, we had to hunt down wild beasts and steal their coats. This concealed, but failed to arrest, the decline and in desperation we took to domesticating sheep, silk worms, dodo birds and long haired slaves — whatever and whomever we could conscript to produce fibres and feathers for fabrics.

Later, we cultivated cotton, flax, hemp, jute and pussy willow and invented machines for spinning, weaving, sewing, cutting and pasting. As a result, we were able to warp and woof our way into the twentieth century, confident that we had finally triumphed over a perverse biology. Alas, the victory was only apparent. As we continued to devolve, natural fibres no longer sufficed, and we had to develop a whole range of synthetics — rayon, nylon, silicon and freon — to mention the most popular. Along the way, we created an exuberant fashion industry to divert attention from our waning resistance to weather. When our resort to fashion failed, we concocted wild theories about global warming

Until recently, we survived without a sophisticated medical system. Oh, we always had doctors and we felt pretty good as long as we stayed away from them. But scientific medicine is really quite new. We saw no need for it when we could look after ourselves with home remedies like chicken soup, hot lemonade and blackstrap molasses. We couldn't do that now. We've dropped so far on the devolutionary scale we demand a hospital in every community and a medical clinic in every shopping centre.

We remained giddily unaware of our declining health until well into the nineteenth century. That's when Louis Pasteur noticed we were vulnerable to germs. It was a turning point. Now, not only germs but viruses, faulty genes and environmental pollutants threaten us from every quarter. We're susceptible to biological, psychological, sociological and tautological ailments that our happy ancestors knew nothing about. Even our spouses make us sick.

Many of us can no longer get through life intact. Our organs tend to wear out before we do. So we have to get by with donated livers, hand-me-down hearts, re-cycled lungs and purloined kidneys. Having to accept other peoples' cast-offs is humiliating, but that's how it is when you're devolving. We're lucky organs are exchangeable. Regrettably, limbs are not. Sometime in our prehistoric past we began riding horses, donkeys, camels, elephants, ostriches and giant land turtles. It was the first sign that our legs were going. We carried on as best we could until a century or so ago, but try as we might we failed to regain locomotive fitness. Out of sheer panic we invented trains, cars, aircraft and motorized golf carts to help us get around. Walking has become increasingly rare and those who persist in it are considered mutants.

We've also experienced mental decline. It, too, began in prehistoric times. That's why we drew pictures of animals on the walls of the caves we lived in. Without visual aids, we couldn't remember what they looked like. It was our first attempt at note taking. Fortunately, our memory for words fared better. Well into historic times we were able to recite the complete works of epic poets like Homer and Virgil by heart. Hearts fail, however, and we eventually had to adopt mental crutches — symbols, alphabets and different forms of writing — to help us remember. It was a sad day for the species when we invented the printing press. It indicated a quantum leap into forgetfulness.

The typewriter, the camera, sound recording and the motion picture and television industries mark recent stages in our creeping amnesia. The computer revolution presages the end of ourselves as we know us. Not only do computers confirm a near absolute failure of human memory. They signal a catastrophic decline in human intelligence as these pushy machines insist on doing our thinking for us. Just as we supplanted large mammals like the woolly mammoth, which went extinct out of sheer pique, so computers are supplanting us. What's more, we seem to be following the mammoth into oblivion. In the developed world, where the devolutionary curve is steepest, the birth rate has been below replacement level for more than a quarter century.

Our latest plan for coping with the devolutionary spiral has been political and economic. Something had to be done about our declining ability to work and earn. We used to be proudly self-supporting. Not anymore. Most of us can't earn enough to survive without government subsidies. The rest can't work at all and have to take government jobs. To solve both problems, we created the welfare state. It's not working either. We don't know why it's not working. Maybe the computers know.

Personality Plus

I REALIZED EARLY ON that I am not fit to be a politician. I was reminded of this when a club I belong to delegated me to secure a politician to address our annual meeting.

"I'm sorry," he said, when I called by his office to invite him. "I have a church service that evening."

"I thought you were an atheist," I said, consulting a dossier the club secretary had prepared for me.

"I am," he replied, "but only in public. In my private life, I'm really quite religious."

I glanced suspiciously at the dossier.

"We were hoping," I said, "that you could explain your support for tighter gun control."

"I only support gun control in the East," he said. "In the West, I'm opposed."

I dropped the dossier into his waste basket.

"Is something wrong?" he asked.

"Politicians are not usually this forthcoming."

"I only dissemble in public," he explained. "In my private life, I'm really quite straightforward."

"Of course," I said. "Why would I think otherwise?"

I had intended to ask him about deficits and debt. But it seemed unnecessary. I expected he would say that while he and his collaborators overspend government budgets, they are fiscally prudent with their own money. I told him so.

"That's correct as far as it goes," he said.

"As far as it goes?"

"A few years ago, I irrevocably opposed deficits for public purposes. Now, I irrevocably support them."

"Did you say irrevocably?"

"It has a different meaning in public discourse than in private conversation."

"You obviously don't think that the personal is political."

"It depends whether I'm thinking privately or publicly," he said.

I was beginning to see that politicians are gifted with split personalities. They may even be gifted with multiple personalities.

"It must be difficult, "I said," for anyone with firm principles to become a politician."

"On the contrary," he said, "without firm principles, no one can become a politician. The first principle of politics is to get elected. The second, like unto the first, is to get re-elected. On these two rest the entire theory of partisan politics. They are the only political absolutes, and they are firm."

"Would you argue that democratic politics is the art of the possible?"

"It depends on the people I'm arguing with."

"But surely it's not the art of the impossible."

"One of my constituents says it's about covering up the consequences of defying reality. If so, it might be the art of the impossible."

"The truth will out, in other words."

"I didn't say that. You did. And what, by the way, is truth?"

I didn't answer. I was eager to know what impact the media have had on politics.

"Dreadful," he said. "The proliferation of audio and video recorders militates against free speech. Some politicians have had no choice but to say the same things in private and in public, in different parts of the country, and from one year to the next. Others have been driven to apologize publicly for things they said privately."

"And to apologize privately for things they said publicly."

"That, too."

"How do you feel when the media misquote you?"

"We don't mind if they misquote us," he said. "We get valuable coverage when we correct them. We do mind if they quote us verbatim."

"You're against accurate reporting?

"Before they had all those recording devices, reporters corrected our grammar, repaired our syntax, and sanitized our language. Now they reproduce what we say word for word, profanity and all.

"I can see how that would discourage free speech."

He picked up an invitation that was lying on his desk.

"I have to leave now," he said. "I'm already late for a vegetarian buffet."

"I didn't know you were a vegetarian," I said.

"I am today," he replied.

He stood up and we shook hands.

"I thought you were much taller," I said, smiling down at him.

"I am, in public. But in my private life, I'm really quite short."

Shoot the Messenger

TAKE ANOTHER LOOK at Canada Post. You probably thought that it's only responsible for the mail. So did I until the postage stamps issued over the last several decades persuaded me that it's also a barometer of our financial health.

I first suspected this in the 1940s, after I started to collect Canadian stamps. Were they boring. Nothing but tiny portraits of monarchs and politicians looking glum. I had Queen Victoria looking dour to the right and grim to the left. I even had a stamp that showed her in widow's weeds, for goodness sake. Oh, there were exceptions. One stamp I rather fancied — it was quite a bit larger than the others — featured a group portrait of the Fathers of Confederation looking glum. Another, an airmail stamp, showed a Canada goose looking listless. I also had a stamp with an RCMP officer on horseback, but the officer just sat there and the horse just stood there. I acquired, as well, a couple of stamps with maps on them, one of the world, the other of Canada, but the maps just lay there.

Those were the days when you could exchange a cereal box top and a few pennies for a packet of foreign stamps. I jumped at the chance and when they arrived I was ecstatic. The stamps, big horizontal and vertical rectangles, were extravagantly colourful and ostentatious, depicting exotic plants and animals that seemed to burst out of their frames. They made my Canadian stamps with their prosaic colours and predictable sizes look like country cousins in hand-me-down clothes. I was embarrassed and self-conscious — typical Canadian traits — but I eventually got over it. This happened as I learned in school about the countries my stamps had come from. Unlike Canada, they were economically backward. Their stamps were colourful and rich, but their people were poor.

It occurred to me that dull, boring stamps might signify staid, conservative leaders. Like the stamps, that kind of leader was unlikely to be undisciplined or intemperate. He wasn't about to get us into financial trouble. Likewise, flamboyant, extravagant stamps might indicate leaders with similar qualities. Oh, I didn't have it all worked out as I do now. I was a young adolescent. But even then I sensed that enterprise, risk taking, innovation and liberality, all profitable virtues in individuals, might degenerate into unprofitable vices in governments.

This was pretty heavy stuff for a lad who weighed not much over one hundred pounds. Nevertheless, from then on I decided to keep an eye on our postage stamps, even after I stopped collecting them. I thought it was the least I could do.

With one worrisome exception, the transition from the 1940s to the 1950s was uneventful. The exception was a stamp showing another Canada goose in flight, only this time it practically soared. I'm afraid it was a bad omen. Later in the decade, several stamps featured hockey players, skiers, swimmers and hunters, all engaged in strenuous activity. They were worrisome, too, but I was reassured by the many portraits of King George VI and

Queen Elizabeth II. They looked as glum as their predecessors.

I kept up a brave front until the mid-1960s, when I thought I detected the hint of a smile on the Queen. I hoped it was one of those rare misprints that collectors pay big money for, but deep down I feared we were headed for trouble. Then the post office issued a colourful series of provincial flowers and my heart sank. They weren't as flamboyant as the foreign stamps that had so intrigued me, but they established a dangerous precedent for even more daring exploits. Their appearance, I later realized, coincided with the beginning of the welfare state in Canada.

The rest of the decade gave me little reason for hope. A portrait of the Governor General was discouragingly jovial. A print of our new flag flying high and proud was depressingly uplifting. A wildlife series looked, if not wild, at least lively, a sports series seemed almost sporty and, more troubling still, a picture of Stephen Leacock revealed that the post office had — would you believe it? — a sense of humour. This was serious.

The 1970s were a decade of special interests and special stamps. The politicians embraced multiculturalism and advertised for disgruntled groups to give our money to. The post office issued stamps commemorating Louis Riel, a rebel, and Nellie McClung, a suffragette. A mountie on horseback reappeared in 1973, but this time he wasn't just posing. He was prancing around in the musical ride. As soon as I saw him, I shouted whoa. It was no use. The national debt started to rise precipitously and the stamps went on to feature flowers and flags in profusion, a host of garish Christmas scenes, athletes in various stages of undress, and a self-serving tribute to mail delivery.

My spirits revived somewhat in the early 1980s. In a fit of nostalgia, the post office issued some reprints from the days when stamps were boring and politicians fiscally responsible, including a reproduction of the mountie asleep on his horse. Shortly afterwards, Canada elected a government that claimed to be conservative. I sat back and waited for the debt to go down.

It didn't, of course. In less time than it takes to lick a stamp, my torturers resumed their wanton ways. They assaulted me with fish, fowl, mammals, insects, flowers and mushrooms. Yes, garish, grotesque mushrooms that practically sprouted out of their frames. Even worse, they dared to present a portrait of the Queen grinning. This was the low point in the decade. The post office was clearly out of control. When I next checked the state of our finances, I saw that the conservatives had betrayed their principles and the debt was rising faster than ever.

In the 1990s, government officials began preaching fiscal restraint. They didn't fool me, though. I couldn't help noticing that after running out of fish, mammals and birds, Canada Post opted for reptiles — dinosaurs, to be exact — and after running out of reptiles, it resorted to legendary beasts like the sasquatch and Ogopogo. I also noticed a series dedicated to dangerous occupations and another depicting popular tales, in which parts of the illustrations really did spill over their frames and onto the borders of the stamps.

Oh, I know that Ottawa has eliminated the federal deficit. I also know that the national debt is as large as ever. Canada Post knows it, too. That, no doubt, is why it spooked investors with a Halloween issue featuring a ghost, a goblin, a vampire and a werewolf.

The government can preach restraint until the sky falls. I won't believe it until I see it in the stamps. Before that happens, the post office will have to tranquilize the Canada goose, put the mountie back to sleep and photograph the Queen sober.

Terra Incognita

I WAS NEVER MUCH GOOD at geography. In high school, two of my classmates told me that Duchabobia was a small country in eastern Europe. They had me believing it was one of the Baltic states, along with Latvia, Estonia and Lithuania. I suppose I should have checked a map, but reading maps didn't come easy to me. It still doesn't.

I even wrote an essay on Duchabobia, filling it with bits and pieces I had picked up in class about the other Baltic states and rounding it out with pure invention. Surprisingly, I received a passing mark. The geography teacher must have believed in Duchabobia, too.

This was not the result my mischievous classmates had intended. They stopped harassing me about Duchabobia, and went on to insist that Gaucamole is a community in Ireland. They said it was featured in the Broadway musical *Finians's Rainbow*. Surely, they said, you must have heard the song "How Are Things in Gaucamole?" Although I had vague memories of a song like that, I knew nothing of Finian or his rainbow. It was news to me that someone could own a rainbow. But, having no reason to doubt the information, I produced another essay.

This was too much for the teacher. To the delight of my persecutors, she refused to mark the essay until I re-wrote it. I now know that Gaucamole is not a community in Ireland. It's a state in Mexico. Glaucoma is the Irish community. If I remember correctly, it overlooks the Islets of Langerhans.

My tormentors next tried to convince me that the monument rising majestically above New York harbour is the Statue of Puberty. They didn't fool me this time, though. I had a particular interest in monuments and knew a thing or two about New York and the Statue of Liberace. I also knew about Paris and the Awful Tower.

Before leaving school, I tried to improve my geographical knowledge by collecting foreign postage stamps. I thought that the exotic birds, animals and scenery the stamps colourfully displayed would motivate me to learn about the countries that issued them. So I traded for stamps from countries like Burma, Ceylon, Nyasaland, Southern Rhodesia, and Tanganyika. Sure enough, the more stamps I acquired, the more geography I learned, but it was to no avail. While inspecting a map of the world recently, I discovered that all those countries have been discontinued. They disappeared following the end of colonial rule, and no doubt took their geography with them. Oh, I know that countries like Myanmar, Sri Lanka, Malawi, Zimbabwe, and Tanzania have replaced them, but it would be too much to expect new nations to put up with old geography. They have to assert their independence.

Despite my geographical limitations, I love to travel. One of my favourite countries is Brazil. I haven't been there, but I became interested in the former Portugese colony through a fondness for Brazil nuts. I also like Macadamia nuts. I haven't been to Macadamia either. Some day I hope to visit both countries.

A few years ago, I had an opportunity to fly to Ireland and check out some of the place names. I also wanted to see the shamrocks. They weren't nearly as interesting as the real rocks. I inspected some of those while scaling the cliffs of Mohair. Although my itinerary included Glaucoma, I had to delete it when I was detained in Dublin doing research into Irish coffee. Then I crossed the Irish Sea to England and visited Sussex, Middlesex and Unisex. They were pretty much as I had imagined them. In London, I made a point of going to Berkeley Square because a nightingale is supposed to have sung there. The trip was a waste of time. There wasn't a nightingale to be seen, or heard, and Berkeley Square turned out to be an oval.

This isn't the first time the travel brochures have disappointed me. One of them promised 362 days a year of sunshine in Palm Springs. I wanted a mere three, as I booked a long weekend in the desert resort to break the trip from Las Vegas to Los Angeles. The first day it rained until nightfall. The second day it snowed. I didn't wait for the third day. Why risk being remembered for using up a year's supply of sunless days in a single weekend?

The brochures also glossed over the earthquakes. An RV park I stayed at in southern California featured a fat New Yorker with a huge sound system, who sat on the roof of his motor home and listened to opera by the hour. The volume was so high the windows in nearby units rattled and you could feel the vibrations. One morning when the earth shook, several of us rushed outside to confront him. But it wasn't his fault. It was the San Andreas Fault. The geology was shifting the geography.

The hacks who write those brochures leave the impression that geography is benign. It's no more benign than history, as anyone can testify who has nearly drowned in "crystalline azure waters", frozen several toes on "sparkling snow-capped mountains", gotten lost in a "primaeval forest's vibrant undergrowth", or run out of gas "midst the dunes of an inscrutable desert". Having seen what revolutionaries can accomplish with revisionist history, these writers are capitalizing on revisionist geography.

Although I have difficulty reading maps, I enjoy looking at them. To me, maps are high art. The continents and oceans on a map of the world are like an impressionist painting. I don't know what it means but I like what it says. What I don't like are the artificial markings the geographers impose on this natural landscape, the parallels of latitude, meridians of longitude, contour lines of elevation and who knows what. I have no use for all that geograffiti.

Hearing is Believing

RADIO enjoyed its finest hours during my boyhood. What I remember best were musical programs from exotic locales that featured big bands with lush arrangements and romantically sounding male and female vocalists.

The announcers always had deep, velvety voices and spoke impeccable English. As they set the scene and introduced the performers they cast an almost hypnotic spell. I don't remember exactly what they said. I do know that I luxuriated in the gorgeous images they were able to evoke. I recall one program in particular that I tuned in to every week.

"Good evening ladies and gentlemen," the announcer would intone creamily. "This is Reginald Gaylord."

Those announcers always had some made-up radio name like Reginald Gaylord or Nathanial Regent. It was enough to make me want to change my own drab name to something more elegant or exciting.

"Welcome," he would continue, " to the Papilloma Gardens."

I'm not sure if that was the right name, but it's close. The only thing Gaylord and the rest had going for them was sound, so the script writers exploited it to the full, dwelling on names and other words that saturated the senses.

"Situated above the sparkling waters of the beautiful Lupus River, the Papilloma Gardens are a riot of springtime blooms, including rubella, chlamydia and pink-eyed susans. In this neuralgic setting, we're delighted to present the sweet and sour music of Jan Stockwell and his Papilloma orchestra."

By then, I was in a trance and nothing short of someone shrieking "fire" could pry me from the radio.

"As the sun sets behind majestic Mount Vertigo, we can hear the evening song of the oral thrush from its nesting grounds in the hills of Catatonia, where the mighty Lupus plunges in cataracts to the plain below, leaving behind it a magnificent spectacle of macular degeneration.

"Just beyond us, in the gathering darkness, lies limpid Lake Scarlatina, where polyps disport themselves and pox, large and small, rise to the sleepy fisherman's bait."

It was like listening to readings from a travel brochure. I begged my parents for a family vacation in one of those exotic places so I could be present at a broadcast like that. They refused to take me seriously, and I never got to meet the men behind the voices or the orchestras behind the music.

"Tonight, we're delighted to feature the vocal renditions of Conrad Sterling and Carlota Powers. Here, Ladies and Gentlemen, accompanied by the Papilloma orchestra are Conrad and Carlota with that perennial favourite 'Melanoma Baby'."

I used to try to imitate those honey-tongued orators in the privacy of my room. I didn't get all the words right, but I had the right spirit, and I went at it by the hour. A few months after my tenth birthday, there was an opportunity to talk on the radio and I seized it. The local station — we had only one in those days — was doing a remote broadcast from the fairgrounds. I arrived an hour ahead of time and was first in line when interviews began with some of the fairgoers.

Although I tried, I wasn't able to sound like Reginald Gaylord. This was a big disappointment. Because of it, I had to forego the pleasure of welcoming the radio audience to the Papilloma Gardens. I talked incessantly, though, as I wasn't the least bit intimidated by the microphone. A technician had to drag me away from it, in fact.

A dozen years later I applied for a job at the same station. As luck would have it, there weren't any openings for studio announcers. Disappointed again, I settled for working in the newsroom, where sounding like Reginald Gaylord was cause for dismissal. Then television arrived, and all those velvety voices and evocative musical programs that lit up my childhood and fired my imagination were quickly gone. I never did get to welcome anyone to the Papilloma Gardens.

But I eventually got to hear Reginald Gaylord in person. He was invited to narrate a review of the golden age of radio at a broadcasters' convention I attended. I sat in the front row and when the spotlight revealed a tall, incredibly handsome gentleman with a physique like a gymnast and luxuriant silver hair, I thought "He's just as I imagined him. That magificent face and body are a perfect match for his deep velvety voice."

I realized my error as soon as he opened his mouth. The voice wasn't deep and velvety. It was shallow and grainy. After a few preliminaries, he introduced a short, scrawny gnome, who was completely bald.

"Reginald Gaylord," he said, as the audience applauded.

This can't be the same Reginald Gaylord, I thought. But when he spoke, there was no mistaking the voice. How such an insignificant body could produce such a substantial sound was beyond me. It was as if a kitten should roar like a lion.

As soon as the house lights dimmed for some film footage, I slipped away. I wanted to retain the rest of my illusions.

One of Me is Enough

THEY SAY that everyone has at least one double and probably several. The wonder is not that some of us look alike. The wonder is that most of us look different. Although nature has relatively few features to work with, among which eyes, noses and mouths are probably the most significant, it has done an incredible job producing millions of faces we can readily tell apart.

I learned quite late in life that I have a double. After decades of assuming that my nondescript appearance was more or less unrepeatable, I was shocked to discover that the template may have been used more than once.

My double was revealed to me in Houston, Texas, while on a bus tour through the Deep South. My wife and I had joined a group of women tourists who were cabbing from our hotel to the nearest Catholic Church for Saturday evening mass. Following the service, I asked the priest if I could use his phone to call a couple of taxis for the return trip.

Looking at me curiously, he seemed hesitant and I wondered if he feared we might try to rob him once we gained entry to the rectory. He consented, however, and after I was done calling he said to the women I was with "I can't get over how much he looks like Alec Guinness."

I didn't know whether to be pleased or annoyed. Did he mean the youngish Alec Guinness, trim and deferential, the middle-aged Alec Guinness, suave and self-assured, or the elderly Alec Guinness, bald and frumpy? I rather suspected it was the last one.

No sooner did he speak than a couple of the women volunteered that they, too, had noticed a resemblance. This guaranteed me a certain notoriety for the rest of the tour and I was conscious of being stared at and whispered about all the way to New Orleans.

Sometimes I played along, adopting what I thought were characteristic Alec Guinness expressions and distinctive Alec Guinness mannerisms. This had absolutely no effect, which is not surprising as I'm not sure it had any purpose. I did it because it seemed the thing to do. I stopped when it occurred to me that the resemblance to my double might be so close it didn't matter which faces I pulled or what poses I struck. I just had to be myself and I was himself.

With that thought, I began to feel like Alec Guinness. Maybe through some mysterious transmigration of souls, or bodies, I was actually becoming Alec Guinness. Maybe Alec Guinness was becoming me. One glance in the mirror dispelled such nonsense. Despite the testimony of the priest and my fellow passengers, I couldn't see much of a likeness. I had no trouble at all telling us apart.

My next run-in with Alec Guinness occurred on another bus tour, this time through the British Isles. An American noted the resemblance and a couple of Australians confirmed it. This was unnerving. It was one thing to look like Alec Guinness in Houston, Texas. It was quite another to do so in London, England, where he lived. At the very least, it was a bit cheeky.

I couldn't help feeling self-conscious. What if some Britishers discovered the similarity and accused me of travelling under false pretenses? What if Alec Guinness himself caught me looking like him? I was embarrassed when a fellow tourist took to calling me Alec.

"Can we join you for lunch, Alec?" "What does Alec think of Stonehenge?" "Move along now, Alec, we're not supposed to taunt the Grenadier Guards." It was enough to make me wish I looked like the Boston strangler.

So, contrary to my behaviour in Houston, I tried not looking like Alec Guinness. I tried hardest at mealtimes, near tourist attractions, in hotel lobbies and around other high traffic areas.

"Are you all right, Alec?" the tourist who had re-christened me asked as we approached the London Palladium. I was trying so hard it was making me ill. If there was one place I didn't want to look like Alec Guinness it was near a theatre he had played at. I couldn't bear the thought of someone asking me for an autograph.

I was ready to swear off bus tours and couldn't wait to return home and regain my anonymity. It was not to be. Back in Canada, a delegate to a convention my wife and I were attending not ten minutes from where we lived came over and said, "Your husband looks like that English celebrity. The name escapes me. Let's see — "

"Vera Lynn?" I suggested.

"An actor, a rather droll fellow," she said. We could see that she wasn't about to quit. To shut her up, my wife quietly volunteered Alec Guinness and we sought refuge in the nearest elevator.

I have since decided that I don't really look like my supposed double. My problem is that Alec Guinness is such a versatile actor and master of disguises he sometimes looks like me.

Law and Literature

LEGISLATION is one of my favourite literary genres. There are few pleasures more satisfying than curling up before the fire with a good statute.

When there's nothing new to read, I often dip into my annotated copy of the Criminal Code of Canada. It provides revealing insights into the character of the Canadian people. You wouldn't believe the trouble we Canadians can get ourselves into. I keep my copy in a secure place. With all that sex and violence, I don't want it to fall into the hands of children.

I also have my very own first edition of The Constitution Act of 1981 and the Charter of Rights and Freedoms. I keep this out of the hands of children as well. All those rights, with not a duty in sight, can be too intoxicating for the immature to handle.

As soon as I get hold of a new law, or an old one I haven't seen before, I don't just read it. I critique its literary qualities. This is a habit I got into as an undergraduate and I can't seem to shake it.

Just as dramatists begin their plays with a cast of characters, legislators start their laws with a list of definitions. Serious readers will pay close attention to these. They provide insight into the action that follows.

Take, for example, the Patent Act, a piece of federal legislation having to do with the protection of inventions.

This Act provides for the appointment of a Commissioner, who is a kind of chief executive officer. Commissioner, the Act says, means Commissioner of Patents. The definition is important; without it, casual readers might assume that the legislation refers to a Commissioner of Oaths or some other such functionary, and miss the point of the story.

Like all legislation, the Patent Act is divided into sections. Under Section 4, we learn that "The Commissioner holds office during pleasure and shall be paid such annual salary as may be determined by the Governor in Council." Did you discern the full import of this? It means that the Commissioner gets paid for having fun. When the fun stops, the job ceases along with the pay. This, of course, is where the plot can take any number of unexpected turns. I dare not reveal more lest I spoil it for you.

But to whet your appetite further, if further whetting is required, I will quote an additional passage, which I think I can do without giving the story away. Subsection 4 of Section 31 says that "where an application is filed by one or more applicants and it subsequently appears that one or more further applicants should have been joined, the further applicant or applicants may be joined on satisfying the Commissioner that he or they should be so joined . . ."

I leave it to feminist critics to denounce the departure from inclusive language. My concern is with the multi-layered meanings of the word joined. If you have any imagination at all, you will have formed a mental picture of an octopus-like creature created by the fusion of several hapless inventors guilty of nothing more menacing than applying for a patent. On this level, the Patent Act seems like a tragedy. But there are deeper levels to which serious readers ought to penetrate. I'll say no more. If you want to follow the story to its gripping conclusion, go to your neighbourhood law library or look it up on the internet. I guarantee that once you've read it, you'll recommend it to your friends.

Like the Bible, the Income Tax Act is universally known and loved, but not often read from cover to cover. I realize that it is very long and that the legion of tangled sub-plots can be difficult to follow; but I assure you that readers who persevere to the end will not be disappointed. Compared to other legislation, the Income Tax Act is a literary tour de force. Since it deals in a special way with the awakening of financial awareness and the first experience of earned income, it is generally regarded as coming-of-age legislation, replete with the tenderness and poignancy characteristic of this genre.

An example is in order. It introduces the concept of tax avoidance, which novice taxpayers must sooner or later confront. As mature readers know, there is a difference between tax avoidance, which has comic overtones and tax evasion, which often ends tragically. But even tax avoidance can end badly if pursued for its own sake, as Subsection 2 of Section 245 deftly illustrates:

"Where a transaction is an avoidance transaction, the tax consequences to a person shall be determined as is reasonable in the circumstances in order to deny a tax benefit that, but for this section, would result, directly or indirectly, from that transaction or from a series of transactions that includes that transaction."

Owing to the exquisite subtlety of this passage, casual readers might fail to realize that the protagonists are losing something they may have thought they were entitled to.

But this bit of literary legerdemain pales to insignificance beside the powerful symbolism embodied in the word transaction. This is not just any action. This is a transaction. Whether or not you know at first reading what it signifies, you cannot help but realize from its constant repetition that it is significant. Every time I read the passage I gain new insight into its significance. I just can't put it into words. Great legislative literature is like that.

Often I read legislation solely for style. What particularly fascinates me are words steeped in subsidiary meanings and nuances. Take, for example, the adverbs hereinafter, heretofore, hereafter, therein and thereafter. Because of their long and noble history, they are able to confer on quite mundane statements a dignity, even a majesty, they would not otherwise possess. All five are splendidly employed in a single sentence of the Saskatchewan Trade Union Act:

"Except as hereinafter provided, every collective bargaining agreement, whether heretofore or hereafter entered into, shall remain in force for the term of operation provided therein and thereafter from year to year."

Upon encountering such expressive prose, the only appropriate response is "I wish I had said that."

Sadly, we don't know who said it. The authors of bureaucratic prose are virtual unknowns. Do you know who wrote the tragic Bankruptcy and Insolvency Act, the comical Young Offenders Act, the exciting Canada Wildlife Act, the mysterious DNA Identification Act, the racy Public Service Staff Relations Act? I thought not. Few of us do.

The reason for this deplorable anonymity is that the authors of these works are uncommonly self-effacing.

Indeed, they are faceless bureaucrats. We can only hope that their disability will soon be protected under the Charter and that they will then feel confident enough to own up to the authorship of an important body of Canadian literature.

We can speed up their acceptance in polite society by insisting that when new legislation is promulgated we hold law launchings and invite the authors to sign copies and give readings. Oh, I know that trained actors are technically better readers. But only the authors themselves can plumb the emotional depth of the material and make it live.

I often fantasize about how wonderful it would have been had the author of the Arctic Waters Pollution Prevention Act given a reading of my favourite passage. It captures the mystery and stark beauty of the Canadian North in a single sentence that, in setting the scene for the drama to follow, describes arctic waters as " . . . the waters adjacent to the mainland and islands of the Canadian arctic within the area enclosed by the sixtieth parallel of north latitude, the one hundred and forty-first meridian of west longitude, and a line measured seaward from the nearest Canadian land a distance of one hundred nautical miles, except that in the area between the islands of the Canadian arctic and Greenland, where the line of equidistance between the islands of the Canadian arctic and Greenland is less than one hundred nautical miles from the nearest Canadian land, that line shall be substituted for the line measured seaward one hundred nautical miles from the nearest Canadian land . . . "

Isn't that breathtaking? Of course it is. I ran out of breath half way through.

Count Me Out *or* Here's Looking at Euclid

MATHEMATICS unnerves me. I have no head for it. I never have had. I can juggle tennis balls. I can't juggle figures. I can balance a billiard cue on my forehead. I can't balance a cheque book anywhere. Sometime between conception and Grade One, I must have been frightened by an odd number or approached by an improper fraction, and it marked me for life. Whenever my teachers would say "Let's go to our number work," I would freeze. I wouldn't thaw out until we went to some other work. To me, all numbers seemed odd, or at least a little strange; all fractions seemed improper, if not downright indecent.

I had enormous difficulty with zeros. I didn't know how many to put down or where to insert the decimal point. The idea of zero — nothing — confused me. I later learned that it's considered one of the most revolutionary discoveries in mathematics. Can you believe that? I can't. How can nothing be revolutionary?

I've read about scientists, inventors and explorers who discovered something. Do you know who discovered nothing? Nobody. Well, nobody we know. Whoever it was apparently lived in India, but his identity is lost in the mists of antiquity. Or is it iniquity? It seems like a sinful discovery for all the trouble it's caused me.

I was the last person in my class to learn how to add and subtract. When the teacher gave me questions in addition. I balked at having to carry figures from one column to another. Let someone else carry them, I told her. When she drilled me in subtraction, I refused to borrow figures from one column for another. I won't go into debt, I said.

After finally mastering those mysterious operations, I took a principled stand against multiplying and dividing. Why, I wanted to know, are there multiplication tables but not division tables? My protests that it was unfair went nowhere. I had little choice but to learn those mysterious operations as well.

By then, my classmates were grappling with fractions, decimals and percentages, and converting one into another. It was more than I could stand. To survive, I made a pact with the best math student in the class that I would write for him if he would figure for me. I made similar pacts throughout elementary and high school. Those pacts plus an aptitude for memorizing what I don't understand kept me going. Luckily, I was always able to find students whose abilities in math were exceeded by their disabilities in English composition.

Even so, my encounters with math were still scary. I felt like fleeing from the room when one of my teachers announced that the equation for finding the area of a circle was $A=\pi r^2$. It was bad enough that math had turned me against numbers. Now, it was going to alienate me from letters.

Next to X, A was my favourite letter. It could say its own name as in take, or denote other sounds as in tack and talk. It could even say another letter's name as in aye, aye, sir. I really liked A, and I was shocked to learn that it had a hidden agenda. I felt betrayed.

But that was only the beginning. As the math got more complicated, letters became as prominent as figures, and none more so than X, my favourite, followed by Y, which I liked almost as much as A. To my horror, I discovered that in algebra and geometry letters shamelessly substitute themselves for all manner of entities and relations, and X is the most disreputable substitute of them all. Indeed, mathematics lives on the avails of substitution. Later, when I heard about $E=mc^2$, Einstein's equation for turning matter into energy, I shed a tear for three more fallen letters.

I suffered another major shock when one of my high school teachers introduced me to a theorem about right angle triangles that some Greek named Pythagoras had developed more than two thousand years earlier. If you square the hypotenuse, the teacher said, it will equal the sum of the squares of the other two sides. The idea of squaring a hypotenuse made me ill. I thought a hypotenuse was a female hippopotamus. I wasn't going to stand by while some sadistic geometrician squared, cropped, whittled or otherwise mutilated one.

After high school, I vowed never again to have anything to do with figures. I was forced to break the vow in university, because I needed a course in statistics to qualify for a teaching certificate. It was an intimidating experience. Right from the start the professor insisted that correlation is not the same as causation. I never said it was. But he made such a fuss over it, now I'm not sure. I always suspect ulterior motives when someone oversells me or is unduly defensive. Then he lectured me about variables. The lucky ones are independent and, I gather, financially secure. The unlucky ones are dependent and, apparently, can't get by on their own.

What all this had to do with getting a teaching certificate I wasn't quite sure. Clearly, it was time to find another math whiz who needed help with his writing.

Grave New World

I'M NOT ONE TO VAULT eagerly into the future. I'm much too comfortable in the past. But this may be about to change. Suddenly, I've become intensely interested in coming events. I guess it's because I've had an apocalyptic vision. Or was it an apoplectic vision? Whatever it was, I've had it.

First, I foresaw a Miss Universe pageant in which the winner was a Canadian. I could scarcely contain my pride when Miss Canada stepped forward and the judges awarded the crown to her plastic surgeon.

"I'm overcome," he said excitedly, the jewelled diadem sparkling on his head. "They said a Canadian couldn't compete against the world's leading medical centres. But our surgical team persevered and after more than fifty cosmetic and reconstructive procedures we produced the beauty you see beside me."

As the audience applauded, he outlined the lifts, tucks, reductions, and augmentations that won the day.

"Before we got hold of her," he said, his eyes moist with suppressed emotion, "she was a mess."

At this, a huge split screen came to life above the stage with before and after images of Miss Canada and glimpses of the surgical team at work on her transformation. As she and her surgeon watched the video, the dazzling smile that had captivated the judges never left her. I'm not sure that it could.

Extensive media coverage followed. What caught my attention were complaints voiced by some of the losing surgeons. They conceded that Miss Canada was the most beautiful candidate. But they argued that in awarding the crown the judges should have given more weight to process than to results.

"Miss Canada may have been a mess," said one. "But you should have seen the hag we had to work with. We improved our candidate far more than they improved theirs."

A reporter asked Miss Canada to comment. She declined. I guess she found it difficult to speak and smile at the same time.

I next foresaw a gala edition of the Olympic Games, in which the athletes performed beyond expectations and human limits and Canada triumphed. Incredibly, more gold medals went to the Canadian pharmaceutical industry than to that of any other country, including the United States and Russia.

Just looking at them, you could tell that the Canadian spectators were ecstatic. The pharmacologists took credit for this, too.

Rallies and parades in every Canadian city paid tribute to our drug researchers and producers. The federal government received accolades as well. Without federal subsidies it would have been impossible to maintain a pharmaceutical edge and ensure that our performance-enhancing chemicals were better than anyone else's.

When asked to comment, a euphoric Prime Minister declared, "Far out."

My vision shifted to an international awards ceremony established to recognize excellence in political, commercial and administrative speech. Government leaders, business executives, and heads of educational institutions were judged on the basis of speeches they had delivered during the past year. Once again Canada came out on top. The jury declared that we had the world's finest ghost writers.

As the Canadian team headed for the stage to pick up their awards, the master of ceremonies quoted excerpts from the best ghost-written speeches of all time. He didn't, of course include anything from the likes of Martin Luther King Jr, Winston Churchill or Abraham Lincoln. Although there's no denying their eloquence, those mavericks were suspected of writing their own material. When challenged about this later, the MC pointed out that the awards ceremony and hall of fame recognized only professionals. "No amateur need apply," he declared, obviously pleased with his choice of words.

Immediately following the ceremony, the winners gave workshops for their fellow ghost writers on such topics as "How to Say Nothing Eloquently", "Excite with Expletives", "Make a Speaker Sound Oxymoronic", "The Art of Ambiguity", and "Rhetoric Trumps Reality".

The event wound up with a cocktail party for the ghost writers and their adoring fans.

"I just love your epigrams," I heard a petite young woman say to one of the winners.

"I'll bet you tell that to all the ghost writers," he replied.

"I do not. Your mixed metaphors thrill me and your syllogisms take my breath away."

"Do you really mean it?"

"Absolutely. I can't get your parentheses out of my mind."

"Please stop. I don't think we should be talking like this in public."

"Maybe we could go somewhere."

Dingwall to the Rescue

MY FRIEND DINGWALL is nothing if not imaginative. He has more good ideas in a year than most people have in a lifetime. If he could implement even a small fraction of them the impact would be revolutionary. He can't, of course. The forces of conservatism and reaction block creative souls like Dingwall at every turn.

Some of his best ideas are in the biological sciences. He's convinced that human evolution went seriously wrong when we stopped growing tails. If only we could stimulate their re-appearance, he told me, we could control obesity once and for all. His idea is to alter human genetics in such a way that any excess fat would accumulate in our rejuvenated tails, which we could periodically amputate according to the dictates of current fashion. A paper he wrote to promote his idea is entitled "Let's Put Obesity Behind Us".

Dingwall's focus on controlling obesity reflects a concern about size in general. An ardent ecologist, he's forever seeking ways of reducing our impact on the environment. One of the best ways, he believes, is through development of an anti-growth hormone.

"We've become too large," he insisted, when I questioned him about it. "Not very long ago, we were much smaller than we are now. Just try putting on a suit of armour from the Middle Ages or a uniform from the

American Civil War. Unless we reverse the trend toward giantism, we'll follow the dinosaurs into extinction."

Dingwall hopes to establish a trend toward dwarfism. He wants us to become a race of midgets or even lilliputians. There's no denying, he says, that the smaller we are the less space we'll occupy and the fewer resources we'll consume. This, in his view, will contribute to harmony among the species.

As soon as we have the anti-growth hormone, Dingwall proposes putting it into the water supply. Once the downsizing begins, he expects that we'll shrink at about the same rate as we previously grew. Besides sparing the environment, the anti-growth hormone will stimulate the economy, since we'll have to downsize the entire infrastructure.

In the meantime, Dingwall remains committed to equality. He's unalterably opposed to adding discriminatory questions about height and girth to the census form. The state, he maintains, has no place in the dining rooms of the nation. Consequently, if Dingwall has anything to say about it, the larger among us will still be allowed to eat in the presence of children, and no one will be prosecuted for growing in public.

Some years ago, Dingwall demonstrated his commitment to equality by launching a spirited campaign for insect rights. It violated his sense of justice to see protesters marching to and fro for cute owls and cuddly seals while sinister forces waged unopposed genocide against the world's least advantaged creatures. He became an advocate of the ant, a brother to the blue bottle fly, a mother figure for the mosquito. He believed that the lowly beetle was the least of his brethren. He opted preferentially for the poor butterfly. "Poor Butterfly", in fact, was his theme song. Dingwall couldn't carry a tune, but he could carry a butterfly.

The benighted masses weren't ready for insect rights. They couldn't see as far as the enlightened Dingwall, and he had to settle for protecting animals and reptiles. So he got some signs made — "Save the Rats", "Take a Lizard to Lunch", "Make Friends with a Skunk" — things like that. He picketed plants that produced pork and mutton and he marched against beef stroganoff, chicken cacciatore, lobster newburg and teriyaki shrimp.

Needless to say, the proponents of dietary preference couldn't fool Dingwall. He was too astute to be taken in by all the rehetoric about protecting gastronomical orientation. He saw at once that it could legitimize cannibalism, and he didn't think there was much to be gained by replacing chicken fingers with the human kind. If this movement succeeds, he told me, it will add new meaning to entrées like Irish stew, Hungarian Goulash and Canadian bacon. Give these crusaders an inch, he said, and they'll take a foot, among other choice cuts.

An important legacy from this period is Dingwall's glossary of specieist words and phrases, which targets human expressions that demean and exclude other creatures. No longer are we to use bug as a verb, as in "Don't bug me." Or flea as an adjective, as in "flea market." Both are offensive to insects. So are such expressions as "fly in the ointment," "bee in your bonnet," and "ants in your pants." Synonyms like chicken for cowardly, bull for falsehood, beef for complaint or bitch for complainer insult domestic animals. To call a dunce a turkey, a glutton a pig or a lecher a goat is especially demeaning, and if committed to paper, such expressions constitute hate literature. Needless to say, Spiderman, Batman and Robin are specieist stereotypes and we should refuse to patronize them.

Dingwall considers it the height of hypocrisy to tout the dog as man's best friend while subjecting it to constant verbal abuse. He therefore proposes to abolish expressions like "dog-eared", "dog tired", "dog days of summer", "dog in the manger", "putting on the dog", "dog-eat-dog world", and "going to the dogs". He also wants us to refuse to stay up until "the last dog is hung" and to stop calling bad poetry doggerel. Our canine companions, he told me, deserve no less.

Before Dingwall became a vegetarian, he briefly owned a cafe. I used to think that the restaurant people had a pretty good idea when they moved the cooking from the kitchen to the dining room. It adds a lot of pizzazz to eating out when you can watch them barbecue your steak at close quarters. It adds even more when you can choose a chunk of meat and barbecue it yourself.

Dingwall had a better idea. He wanted to add a slaughter house and butcher shop so you could choose your steak on the hoof and follow it through to the table. If you were so inclined, you could even do your own butchering.

The local bureaucrats would have none of it. They threatened legal action and put Dingwall under surveillance. Then — wouldn't you know it? — they looked the other way when a couple of their political cronies stole the idea. They installed some aquariums, stocked them with lobsters and crabs, let the diners choose the ones they liked, and slaughtered, butchered and cooked them on the premises. This kind of thing happens to my friend all the time.

Dingwall's latest idea is another winner. He proposes to solve the problem of second-hand smoke without prohibiting the use of tobacco in public. At the same time that we ban it for smoking, he told me, we must vigorously promote it for chewing.

"Chewing is a lost art. The sooner we reinstate it, the healthier and safer our communities will be. We'll have a smoke-free environment without denying tobacco users the considerable benefits they derive from nicotine."

Just thinking about it filled me with nostalgia. As a pre-schooler, I used to accompany my father, a travelling salesman, on weekly trips throughout the province. One of my most vivid memories is of the gleaming gold spittoons that graced the lobbies of the hotels we stayed at. The expert marksmen who used them were among my boyhood heroes. I can still see their arching missiles glistening amber in the afternoon sun. I can still hear the liquid tones as each found its target. Those gleaming vessels are gone now, rendered virtually obsolete by the success of the cigarette industry. Occasionally, you see them in antique shops, but anonymous purchasers eager to re-live a glorious past snap them up almost as soon as they appear.

If Dingwall has his way, they'll become as common as ash trays recently were. Perhaps even more so, as women increasingly exercise their freedom to chew. Equality of the sexes, Dingwall believes, will revolutionize the art of expectoration. It will also, no doubt, have an impact on the design and production of spittoons, as manufacturers strive to accommodate a feminine clientele. Beaming, Dingwall confided that we could soon see a renaissance in cuspidorial art. I think it's his best idea yet.

Take a Bus

YOU HAVEN'T REALLY TRAVELLED until you've done a bus tour. There's nothing in the world like a two- or three-week romp in the close company of forty or more perfect strangers, whose names you can't remember and whose ailments and personality quirks you can't forget.

What we call a bus in North America is a coach in Britain. It amounts to the same thing, though, except that a bus usually has a lavatory at the back and a coach may not. Bus riders tend to use it only as a last resort. I suspect it offends their aesthetic sense, not to mention their sense of smell when it malfunctions. So whether you're on a bus or a coach, periodic rest stops can become an obsession. Since no smoking is allowed, you make common cause with the nicotine addicts in promoting a liberal number of comfort breaks. This becomes increasingly important as the tour proceeds and the ingestion of unfamiliar food and drink takes its toll.

Most buses have a crew of two, an operator who can drive through the eye of a needle, and often does, and a tour director who provides a running commentary and enforces the rules. A key rule is seat rotation. Once a day you're supposed to change places, moving counter-clockwise down one side of the aisle and up the other. This ensures equal exposure to the best views and the worst talkers.

A bus tour is not the sedentary vacation you might imagine. You get plenty of exercise, regular and irregular. To pass your fellow travellers in the aisle, you have to pull in your stomach and straighten your legs. To access carry-on luggage in the compartments above or on the floor below, you have to stretch your arms and bend your back. To glimpse the scenery on both sides of the bus, you have to crane your neck and swivel your head. All of which is in addition to rotating your seat.

The exercise intensifies as the carry-ons grow fatter and heavier with each day's shopping and the struggle to stow them securely grows nastier. Thank goodness the serious luggage is the responsibility of the driver and hotel porters, who stow it under the floor. These bags grow fatter and heavier, too, and experienced observers can tell what stage a tour is at from how much the bottom sags, on the bus and on the driver.

Even when everyone speaks the same language, communication can be a problem. One group I travelled with included residents of England, Ireland, Scotland, Wales, Australia, New Zealand, Canada and the United States. A woman told me that she had a hard time understanding most of them.

"I don't know what to say in reply," she lamented. "They talk so fast I can't decipher their accents,"

"Say anything you like," I counselled her. "Only you talk fast, too, and they won't be able to decipher your accent."

"I don't have an accent," she said. "I'm Canadian."

Bus tours attract mainly the elderly, most of them married couples. Widows far outnumber widowers, as they do among seniors generally. On a recent tour, a widow told me that she was spending her late husband's money. She added cheerily that my wife would likely end up doing the same. I thanked her on behalf of my wife and promised to keep saving.

Not only have many bus tourists survived their marriages. Virtually all have survived one or several ailments that have incapacitated or eliminated their peers. Their luggage is stuffed with prescription and over-the-counter drugs and they're ready to recite their medical histories at the pop of a pill. If you're imprudent enough to ask them how they are, you can expect a dissertation.

They're survivors, all right, and they're determined to survive the bus tour. You hear them gasp for breath as they crest an Arizona mountain or groan in pain as they bump and jerk along an Irish rural road. They think nothing of descending into the Carlsbad Caverns and getting lost among the stalagmites or hobbling several storeys up an ancient spiral staircase and dislocating a vertebra trying to kiss the Blarney Stone. I've seen an 80-year old set out alone at night to explore the French Quarter in New Orleans and an 83-year old, cane in hand, challenge the Cliffs of Moher.

Sophisticates are apt to dismiss bus tours as tame, confining and boring. They're not. Adventure is never far away. What can be more adventurous than having the bus break down in the middle of the Mojave Desert? There are few things as thrilling as beating your bus mates to a cactus large enough to squat behind. What can be more exciting than having your driver get lost in the innards of New York City? There are few things as diverting as watching your crew exit the bus in the black of night to ask directions of a clump of lounging locals.

What, pray tell, can be more thrilling than stepping off the bus in a Palestinian village and bobbing and weaving to avoid being shot? Not by snipers, you fool, by amateur photographers. Like virtually all travellers, most bus tourists are camera buffs. I find them intrusive and threatening. I can't fully enjoy the grandeur of Rome or the quaintness of London while having constantly to be on guard against walking into someone's picture and incurring the menacing looks, gestures and remarks that inevitably follow. I resent having to spoil my holiday in order to avoid spoiling someone else's photograph.

I never carry a camera. Only once have I regretted this. I was on a bus tour in The Highlands of Scotland, when we stopped by a field of heather. I stayed aboard while my travelling companions dutifully trooped out and formed a long single line with their backs to the bus and their cameras blazing. When they'd finished shooting, they all bent over in unison to grab some heather for souvenirs. What a picture that could have made. I would have captioned it "seat rotation".

Have a Nice Day

AS FAR AS I'M CONCERNED, weather is about things like temperature, humidity and air circulation. That's not enough for most people, however. For as long as I can remember, they've personified the weather and in recent years, they've deified it. As in olden days, they've invested it with supernatural attributes.

One of my most enduring memories from primary school is of a textbook sketch showing the sun as a happy face and the wind as a disembodied head with inflated cheeks. I blame that sketch for many a painful burn because I trusted the sun to live up to its image and treat me gently. It didn't. Neither did the wind. I thought that hoary old man might have been blowing out candles on a birthday cake. It never occurred to me that he had enough air in his cheeks to tear the roof off my playhouse.

You'd think tornadoes were gifted with intellect, will and emotion the way journalists go on about them. I've seen them portrayed as cunning and arrogant as they cruelly decide to attack one community while sparing another. It's a wonder we don't haul them before a human rights tribunal for unfair discrimination. I've seen the western jet stream described as the culprit in a string of country-wide low temperatures that upset an entire nation. It's a wonder we don't lay criminal charges.

Are these capricious weather systems playing with us, the scribes ask. Are they acts of God? Whatever the answers to such rhetorical questions, we seem to have projected onto these unruly systems the trappings of the pagan gods and goddesses of our mythological past.

I became acutely aware of this deification of the weather one depressing prairie summer when we endured unsettled atmospheric conditions for more than a month. This, of course, set off all sorts of fanciful speculations. The most intriguing was that we were reaping a form of retribution. It was payback time, the weather watchers suggested, for earlier winters that were abnormally mild. The weather, they were implying, was meting out justice, like Zeus atop Mount Olympus.

When the atmospheric conditions changed, exposing us to several days of stable, warm air, some cried, "We deserve this." It was as if through adversity they had merited a measure of godly favour. Others, filled with solemn gratitude, refused to protest the loss of a substantial part of their summer. By suffering silently, they thought that they could placate the weather and avoid future ill treatment, just as the ancients thought that they could placate their sometimes vindictive gods.

It pains me when picnickers scan a darkening sky and exclaim, "Please don't rain!" Do they really believe that the weather hears their petitions? It troubles me when composers pen hymns to the weather: "Here Comes the Sun"; "Let it Snow, Let it snow, Let it Snow"; "With the Wind and the Rain in Your Hair"; "Baby, it's Cold Outside." Do they really believe that the weather cares?

And what about the scriptures that have coalesced around the state of the atmosphere, the weather lore that persists from age to age? Granted, it's poetic and sometimes predictive, but must we continue to take it seriously?

We're all familiar with at least some of it: A ring around the moon means that rain is coming soon; Rainbow in the eastern sky, the morrow will be dry; Year of snow, crops will grow; Sound traveling far and wide, a stormy day will betide. The best I can say about these silly verses is that they are about as reliable as the silly prose the TV weathercasters mouth daily.

In the hierarchy that presides over our weather worshipping community, the theoretical meteorologists are at the pinnacle. They are the theologians of this ersatz religion, striving mightily to unlock the secrets of the atmosphere. They were doing all right until one of them asked the intriguing question: Does the flap of a butterfly's wings in Brazil set off a tornado in Texas?

This ignited all sorts of collateral speculation: Might a sneeze in Saskatchewan cause a hurricane in Haiti? Will a bout of the hiccups in Harlem produce a series of typhoons in Thailand? Can we blame a flatulent cow in California for a blizzard in Boston?

The so-called Butterfly Effect, not to mention the Bovine Effect, severely challenged meteorologists. They had to admit that the weather, unlike the people who announce it, might be inherently unpredictable, because it can be influenced by something as minor as a cow breaking wind.

Below the theoretical meteorologists are the prophets who plot the short- and long-range forecasts. Like all prophets, they speak a language that lay people have difficulty deciphering. Who, for example, can tell a cumulonimbus from a circumlocution? Who knows the difference between an isobar and a mini-bar? Who cares? But that's all right because the media weathercasters, the evangelists mandated to spread the word, are adept at translating meteorological jargon into the *lingua franca* of gossip. Masters of small talk, the smaller the better, they seek to entertain as well as inform and often fail to do either. If a forecast turns out right, they take the credit; if it goes wrong, they blame the forecasters. "We're just the messengers," they protest, when a predicted mild spell gives way to a blizzard.

I find that they're best at reviewing yesterday's weather. They get that right most of the time. They're also pretty good as describing current conditions. Beyond that, their performance is mixed, if not mixed up. It's as if there were a butterfly in the ointment, or a cow unwinding in a distant pasture.

There's Something about the Irish

THE MORE I LOOK INTO IT, the prouder I become of my Irish heritage. Throughout history, social commentators have spoken about us Irish in superlatives — the most, the greatest, the best, that sort of thing. Why, just the other day I read that Strabo, the early Greek geographer, considered us the most barbarian people in the world. Nineteen hundred years later, the inhabitants of at least three continents included us among the greatest drinkers and the best brawlers.

Our drinking and brawling, in fact, are memorialized in two surviving institutions: the donnybrook, a riotous free-for-all, and the Paddy wagon, a jail on wheels.

In Elizabethan times, the English considered us white savages. I'm not sure I know the difference between a savage and a barbarian. The English no doubt know. They had ample time to ponder the question during the centuries in which they relieved us of our troublesome independence and deepened the poverty that came natural to us.

Under their protection, we trimmed our numbers by a million during the potato famine of the 1840s. Potatoes were our principal, sometimes our only, food. If we were lucky, we ate them three times a day. If not, we ate them twice, once or not at all. When the potatoes disappeared, so did many of us.

By all accounts, our poverty was unique, another superlative. You may have heard of people who handed down clothes from one generation to the next. We handed down rags from one generation to the next. French writer Gustave de Beaumont found our situation more extreme than that of American Indians and blacks. The average life expectancy of southern slaves was 36, of Irish peasants, 19. So you see we were special.

We immigrated to other countries by the millions, causing our population at home to decline for generations, something few nations can boast of. We were a gregarious people and we remained so both at home and abroad. In Ireland, England and the United States, we welcomed pigs, chickens, and other living creatures into our homes, and kept them there, even in towns and cities.

Wherever we journeyed, we made an impression on the people we lived among, particularly in the United States. Early on, some of us became hard-drinking frontiersmen, the Indian fighters who led the westward advance. Others settled in eastern mountain valleys, where our descendants became hillbillies and provided inspiration for cartoonists. Later, we moved into urban slums, where police stopped by in groups, often to give us rides in their Paddy wagons.

When we crowded into Boston in the 1840s, the number of saloons rose by almost fifty percent in three years. Some observers got the impression that we'd rather play than work. Employers in major American cities respected this, often putting up help wanted signs that specified no Irish need apply. They weren't nearly so considerate of blacks, whom they frequently hired ahead of us. When we settled in a neighbourhood, others often kindly moved out, leaving us to establish our communities unhindered. Neighbours who refused to move for blacks were happy to do so for us.

Historically, we weren't much interested in formal education. We were the only European nation not to build a university during the middle ages. We also had little time for business, preferring to work for others. In America, our men tended to take unskilled jobs that were hard, menial and dangerous; our women generally went into domestic service. Southern masters often hired us to do work they considered unsafe for slaves. Slaves, after all, were valuable property. Paddies were expendable.

Although indifferent to work, we were spirited at play, especially play on words. Our wit and oratory are legendary and we produced literary luminaries out of all proportion to our numbers. This despite having abandoned our native tongue, Gaelic, for the language of our protectors.

Our facility with words, together with our vivacity and good fellowship, created opportunities in politics. By the late nineteenth century, Irish political machines dominated many American cities. We also rose to prominence in labour unions and came to control the Roman Catholic Church in the United States and Canada.

Not only did we lose our language along the way, we eventually lost much of our culture, especially the drinking, brawling, ignorance and indolence that spared us the burdens of wealth. The Church bears a heavy responsibility for the disappearance of these traits and for our assimilation into the culture of the majority. If now there is little to distinguish us from most others in wealth and social status, I guess the Church is at least partly to blame.

But, generally speaking, we're a forgiving people and don't hold grudges, at least not outside our ethnic group. Since adopting the attitudes, values, habits and skills that all peoples require for economic advancement, we seem content to let bygones be bygones. I don't know of any Irish proposals for preferential treatment to compensate for centuries of exploitation and deprivation at home and abroad. I haven't met any Irish who want to sue Church and State for collaborating in our assimilation by the societies we immigrated to. I guess it doesn't make sense to us Irish to blame our compatriots for what their forebears did. I certainly wouldn't want anyone to blame me for what my forebears did.

Political correctness is not one of our strong points, I'm afraid. In *The Nonsexist Word Finder*, Rosalie Maggio provides what she believes are acceptable substitutes for words and phrases that may be offensive in the context of gender, race and ethnic origin. For black Maria, possibly doubly offensive, she proposes Paddy wagon. It apparently hasn't occurred to her that this might offend the Irish, but that's all right because it probably hasn't occurred to us that we might be offended.

In deference to their Irish Catholic community, Liverpudlians have nicknamed an architecturally unusual church Paddy's wigwam. In North America, such a sobriquet would attract protests from the aboriginals, but not from the Irish. On a visit to Liverpool, I got lost looking for the church and, in asking directions, felt completely safe referring to it by nickname.

But this is to be expected. We Irish pride ourselves on our repartee and have always been able to come up with apt nicknames, poetic images and metaphors. Why should we object when someone else does the same?

Let others complain when their racial or ethnic origins are celebrated in the names of athletic teams and restaurants. It doesn't mean that we have to. I'm rather proud when someone calls a team the Fighting Irish or a restaurant the Green Leprechaun.

Thank goodness we didn't have to endure affirmative action and other demeaning programs designed for historically disadvantaged groups. Schemes like that could have sapped our initiative and we might still be dining on potatoes, drinking and brawling the way we used to, and languishing in ignorance and indolence. You might call our escape from such programs the luck of the Irish.

Canine Capers

THEY EAT HORSES, DON'T THEY? Indeed, they do. In the wake of mad cow disease, horse meat is becoming increasingly popular in Europe. When a European is really hungry and cries "I could eat a horse," the chances are that he will. I've never tasted horse, but I know people who have, and they enjoyed it. A touring musician I once befriended used to regale me with stories about inviting acquaintances for a steak or roast dinner and, after receiving their compliments, informing them that under different management the meat they had just consumed won the daily double.

Not everyone is comfortable with the idea of biting into a Shetland sandwich or munching a Pinto burger. Frankly, the thought of marinated Mustang or Palomino patties doesn't do anything for my appetite. On the contrary, it makes me nauseous.

But that's just a cultural hang-up. With proper conditioning, I could learn to consume horse meat with the same gusto I now eat beef and recoil from beef with the same intensity I now shrink from horse meat. Which is all to the good, because if mad cow disease becomes entrenched, we meat eaters may have to resign ourselves to a world without beef and look to other mammals to satisfy our carnivorous cravings.

I suggest dogs. If turning steeds into steak doesn't interest you, consider turning hounds into hamburger. In parts of Asia, people think nothing of biting into a juicy dog. That can't be worse than in North America, where dogs think nothing of biting into a juicy person. I've been bitten by a dog and, believe me, I'd have rather not. If I had to choose between chewing on a dog or having a dog chew on me, I'd change my diet in a minute.

Oh, I know that dogs are companion animals and to dine on your companions might seem a little like cannibalism. But pigs and lambs can be companion animals, too, and few of us object to dining on pork or mutton. We tend to raise companion animals and livestock separately, allowing the companions inside and keeping the others out. It wasn't always this way. Many of our forebears used to open their homes to goats, geese and other edible creatures and consider it normal. Our ancestors didn't always distinguish between pets and provisions. We don't need to either. Pet food doesn't just mean food for pets. It can also mean pets for food.

If only we knew it, we all have a subconscious urge to taste German Shepherd's pie, Irish Setter stew, rack of Rottweiler, baked Alaskan Malmute or any of the other canine recipes leading chefs are capable of developing. But because the urge is socially unacceptable, we either repress it and live with unresolved frustration or sublimate it and eat hot dogs. Psychiatrists call the tendency to be gastronomically aroused by our dogs the Eatapup complex. It originates in infancy, no doubt because babies are programmed to put anything that attracts their attention into their mouths, and dogs are programmed to attract attention. I recognize the complex in myself whenever the yappy terrier across the way keeps me awake at night and I feel like biting off one of its hind legs.

In a psychiatrically correct world, we would no longer repress or sublimate a passion for Chihuahua chowder. If visiting friends were to ask, "Where's Fido?" it wouldn't seem strange to reply, "He's in the freezer." If dinner guests were to inquire over cocktails, "What's that delicious aroma?" it would feel perfectly normal to reply, "That's Rex. He'll be done in less than fifteen minutes."

It's time we stopped discriminating against dogs when we plan our menus. Dogs have as much right as any other animal to grace our dinner tables. The dog, we are told, is man's best friend. Is it not peculiar that we include in our diets cattle, sheep, pigs, chickens and turkeys, many of which are not even acquaintances, and yet exclude our best friends? Shame on us.

In the interests of rooting out this nasty prejudice, I have devoted a significant part of my life — all of fifteen minutes — to researching recipes aimed at inspiring dog fanciers to see their relationships in a new light. If I am successful, the exclamation "I love dogs" will be analogous to "I love shrimp", "I love Cornish hens", "I love suckling pigs", or whatever delicacy we might be moved to pronounce on. Consider the following:

CANINE CACCIATORE

1 dog, cut up; 1 c regular rice, uncooked; 1 can diced tomatoes with juice; 1 sm. can mushroom pieces; 1 can cream of mushroom soup plus 1 can water; 1 tbsp. chopped pimento; 1/2 pkg. dry onion soup

Put all ingredients (except dog) into pan; stir together, then place dog on top. Sprinkle with paprika, salt & pepper to taste; dot with oleo. Bake 1 hr. at 325 degrees (covered), then uncover and bake another 30 minutes.

SUGGESTED WINES

Anything with a bite.

Night Life

I WAS IN THE BAR enjoying an afternoon drink when one of the patrons fell asleep and started snoring. It was a remarkable performance, raucous and intimidating. I hadn't heard anything quite like it before. Neither, apparently, had the bartender, who woke up the perpetrator and sent him on his way. Another patron — he looked like a wizened old sea captain — moved over beside me.

"I've heard lots better than that," he said, nodding toward the departing barfly. "Years ago, I was night watchman at a hostel on the lower west side, where guys travelling on the cheap used to spend a night or two in the dormitory. I heard a lot of snoring and I got to be an expert on the subject."

"Not many people would have that opportunity," I said. I had some time to spare and I didn't mind the intrusion.

"I remember a big lumber jack. When he breathed in, he would trumpet like an elephant."

"How odd," I said, intrigued as much by the intensity of his delivery as by the content of the story.

"Yeah, and when he breathed out, it was like a flatulent cow."

"He was the champion," I suggested.

"Hell, no. There were lots better than he was. There was a magazine salesman who put so much energy into his snoring he exhausted himself every half hour or so and stopped breathing 'til he turned blue. When he finally inhaled, it was like a car breaking to avoid a collision."

"Incredible."

"Yeah, and there was a professional wrestler who used to pop every light bulb in the dorm. It was a physics thing. Something about compatible frequencies."

"Or incompatible frequencies."

"Who knows? Anyhow, I had to sweep the floor so the other sleepers didn't cut their feet when they got out of bed."

"Was he the champion?"

"Not on your life. The best individual snorer I ever heard — you can't compare individuals and teams — was a 300-pound bouncer with a chest as big as a cistern. He snorted like a pig when he took on air and whinnied like a horse when he expelled it, waking himself up at ten-minute intervals. Every so often, he'd sleep through for a while, letting the sound build, and you'd swear he was a jet revving his engines on the runway. I had to wear earplugs and my nose bled intermittently all night."

"That must have been terrible," I said.

"It wasn't so bad. Some of the sleepers in the other beds lost control of their sphincter muscles. But it was worth it just to hear a real champion at work. He stayed with us a few nights and demonstrated quite a repertoire. He was no single-note snorer, let me tell you. There were times you'd swear a police car was careening by, its horn alternating in pitch like you hear on TV. And he could snore equally well both ways."

"Both ways?"

"Yeah. His soft palate vibrated as much when he exhaled as when he inhaled. Sometimes he'd settle down to a steady roar like one of those gas mowers people cut their lawns with Sunday afternoons. Let me tell you, I won't hear the likes of him again. Not if I live 'til I shrink."

He looked as if he'd shrunk already, but I didn't have the heart to mention it.

"Do you think good snoring is innate or acquired?" I asked.

"Both," he said, decisively. "It's partly in the genes. In the first place, you've got to be big and strong. In the second place, you need a cavern for a chest cavity and leather lungs. The mouth, nose, soft palate and airways are important, too. Subtle differences can separate the champions from the duffers. But all that doesn't matter much if you don't get plenty of regular practice. I never met a married man who could snore to his full potential."

"Marriage discourages snoring?"

"Yeah. Their wives are always waking them up and turning them over, or stuffing rags in their mouths so they can only breathe through the nose. You can't develop into a champion with that kind of interference."

"Wives don't appreciate the finer points of snoring, I guess."

"I never knew a woman who could snore worth a damn," he said. "It's probably an evolutionary thing."

"Men evolved to be better snorers?" How, I wondered, had Charles Darwin overlooked this.

"Yeah, men were the protectors. When the family was asleep and vulnerable in their caves, the snoring frightened away wild beasts."

"But why the men, why not the women?"

"The men started out bigger and stronger and they developed from there. The women never caught up. They don't have the airways for it or the upper body strength, and their lungs aren't powerful enough. They're not as aggressive as men, or as reckless."

"Reckless?"

"Yeah, I've known men who snored themselves to death"

"What on earth could cause that?"

"Oh, their lungs gave out, or they burst a blood vessel, or maybe choked. One guy exploded."

"How did you feel when it happened on your watch?"

"Not so bad. None of those guys was championship material."

He sensed that I was ready to leave and put a hand on my arm. "I haven't told you about the teams," he said. "You can't really appreciate snoring until you've heard a team do their stuff."

"You mean to say people collaborate in this?"

"Not consciously, I suspect. But when a group sleeps in the same room a lot they tend to synchronize their efforts. I had a bunch of Swedish hitchhikers who co-ordinated their snoring into a steady purr. It was low-pitched, but loud enough to be heard outside. Those Swedes had every stray cat in the neighbourhood scratching on the doors trying to get in."

"Are you suggesting that ethnic or cultural differences affect how we snore?"

"As far as I'm concerned they do. I had a group of Italians who were as different from the Swedes as night is from day. They snored in four-part harmony the whole time. What a performance. They sounded like one of those gigantic pipe organs and you could hear them all over the west side. They started off quietly enough, but by the time they were in full snore, they raised the roof. I mean that literally. The next morning, I had to bring in the carpenters."

"Did you have any female teams?"

"Women can't cut it collectively, either. One of them is sure to start talking in her sleep. Another answers, and before you know it they're all taking their turn and they've barely enough energy left to breathe, let alone snore."

He stopped just long enough to finish his drink and was off again before I could ask what the women talked about.

"But the Italians," he said, "they couldn't approach the performance of an Irish group I had in one night. No sir. When those Irishmen snored in unison, they inhaled such enormous gulps of air it created a near vacuum. The imbalance between the outdoor and indoor pressure caused the rafters to creek, the walls to bend, and my ears to pop. I had to open the doors to prevent the foundation from cracking."

"What happened when they exhaled?"

"They blew the doors shut, so I had to tie them open."

"It's a wonder the hostel survived."

"Well, it didn't. On a return visit they generated such powerful vibrations, the building collapsed on top of them. They just kept on snoring in the rubble and didn't stir 'til sun-up. Yeah, that was the end of the hostel and the end of my job. I didn't care one bit. No sir. When those big Irishmen got up and dusted themselves off, I just stood and cheered, and then I shook hands with every one of them. What's a job compared to a performance like that? Who else can tell his grandkids he was there when those crazy Irishmen brought down the house?"

Deal Me Out

IT'S A GOOD THING I'm not in business. I have no head for it. Business people make money. I can't do that. I don't have the ingredients. If I had them, I wouldn't know what to do with them. When I was growing up, bankers created money with the stroke of a pen. I didn't have a pen like that. Now they do it with the stroke of a key. My computer doesn't have a key like that. Since I can't make money, I have no choice but to earn it. This is where business people have it all over me.

An economist recently told me that money is basically debt. No wonder I'm not rich. I always thought debt was something I should avoid. If I got into it, I couldn't wait to get out. Well, the economist said, if everyone thought like that, we'd be poor as hillbillies. Having abolished debt, we'd have no money. Business people know this instinctively. The successful ones go into debt until they're wealthy. That's the difference between them and me. They know how to borrow their way to prosperity. I don't.

It's not only that I can't make money. I can't lose it. I've tried, but my heart isn't in it. Business people lose money enthusiastically — not their own, other peoples'. I suspect that's how they borrow their way to prosperity. While losing other peoples' money, they make their own. Of course, it helps if they can go bankrupt at the proper times. Some of the richest people I know started out by losing everything they borrowed. Once they mastered that, their fortunes were made.

Business people are fiercely independent. I admire that. There's nothing like being independent, especially if you're fierce. Typically, they're self-made men. I admire that, too, because there's no way I could have made myself. I wouldn't have known where to begin. Making myself, I suspect, would have been harder than making money. With business people, it's as easy as going bankrupt.

Independence, fierce or otherwise, is their most valuable asset. To maintain it, they depend on loans, grants and creative tax concessions. Private enterprise and free competition are valuable, too. To support private enterprise, business people get public subsidies; to safeguard free competition, they get the government to limit pesky competitors. As you may have gathered, business people have a cozy relationship with politicians. I don't know how they manage it. I've never met a politician I felt like getting cozy with.

When people go into business, chances are they'll become employers and have to deal with employees. Employees can be counted on to steal from the business. They do it on principle. The bad ones rob their employers blind. The good ones rob them, too, but only until they can't see straight. Shrewd employers respond by reducing staff. They automate, integrate, fumigate, detonate — whatever it takes. This is known as down-sizing and is aimed at securing a labour-free work place.

To succeed in business, they need to show a profit. They don't actually have to produce one, just show it. This is what accountants are for. They can show pretty well anything, including losses. When called upon, they can show profits and losses at the same time. This is known as double entry bookkeeping and is aimed at reporting profits to appease shareholders and losses to confound tax collectors. More commonly, it's called funny business, a term of endearment which recognizes that contrary to appearances, accountants have a wicked sense of humour.

Business, unfortunately, has its detractors. You may have heard that business people are committed to maximizing profits, regardless of the consequences. That's not true. Whatever happens, they only want to get as much as they can. You may have heard that they're avaricious. That's not true either. The worst you can say about them is that they're greedy. You may have heard that they crave power. They do not. They just want to be in control.

The critics tend to overlook their contributions. Take the business cycle, for instance. What could be more socially significant than alternating routinely between boom and bust? Resonating with the rhythms of nature, they're the economic expression of yin and yang, wax and wane, to and fro, over and out. Take advertising, for another instance. Without it, we couldn't afford to watch television, read newspapers, put up colourful billboards along highways, overpay athletes. Take, finally, inequalities in wealth. Without them, we wouldn't have business people to envy.

They say there's no longer any romance in business. It's all about growing bigger and getting richer. Well, I'm not so sure. During lunch the other day, I overheard an intimate conversation between two business people of the opposite sex. As nearly as I can remember, here's what happened.

"I see your stock is on the rise," he said. "It increased three percent today alone."

"I didn't think you'd notice," she said, blushing.

"How could I not notice? I own a block of it."

"Do you really?"

"I certainly do. The price was right and I needed another equity to balance my portfolio. I couldn't resist."

"I'll bet you say that to all the business girls."

"I don't, honest I don't. You're way ahead of the others. Not only are your assets undervalued. You're diversified and your debt-to-equity ratio is attractive."

"Please. You're embarrassing me."

"But it's true. Efficiency, productivity, entrepreneurial verve. You've got it all."

"I don't think we should be talking this way. We hardly know each other."

"On the contrary, I've been watching your bottom line for months. It's very nice."

"Really? Why didn't you say something sooner?"

"I didn't want you to think I was trying to engineer a hostile takeover."

"That's very considerate of you. I like that in a business man. I like it a lot."

"Do you? Then perhaps you wouldn't mind if I — " He paused trying to come up with the right way of saying it.

"Don't be bashful," she said. "I'm hanging on your every word."

This gave him the courage he needed.

"I know there are risks even bringing it up, and you needn't answer right away, but I'm hoping that sometime in the near future you might be open to, to a merger."

She started to cry.

"Oh, forgive me," she said. "I'm really touched. You don't know how much this means to me."

"Well, actually, I do. I completed a financial analysis only yesterday."

At this, she collapsed in his arms, overcome with emotion.

"I don't know what to say," she blubbered, "except that you've got a nice bottom line, too."

"You really think so?"

"I know so. I completed my financial analysis last week."

United We Burn

WHEN I WAS A BOY, my companions pretended to be firemen, policemen, spacemen, prosaic things like that. Not me. I pretended to be a union man. I became obsessed with unions the first time I saw a labour demonstration. I desperately wanted to join in. I wanted to march to and fro waving a placard. I wanted to stop traffic and hand out leaflets. I wanted to build a fire in a barrel and burn someone in effigy.

When they run out of things to say, adults often ask children what they're going to be when they grow up. Visitors to our house were no exception.

"A shop steward," I would reply and give them the union salute. Well, I thought it was a salute. I'd seen the demonstrators give it to a courier who crossed their picket line.

I managed to get into the labour movement before I grew up. I joined the musicians' union when I was fourteen. It was the only union a minor could belong to in our city. What a thrill to attend my first meeting and call the other members brother this and sister that. What a joy to blacklist my brothers and sisters when they worked for less than union scale. What a delight to boycott non-compliant dance halls, to harangue radio stations for using recorded music without paying the performers, to complain generally about our place in the social order. We were like a big, unhappy family.

It wasn't all fun though. For one thing, I had to take up a musical instrument. Even worse, I had to learn the stupid thing and play dances and other tiresome gigs. I had no choice. I needed the money to pay my union dues. I took up the trumpet. What an ordeal. But it was worth it just to be able to stand beside my brothers and sisters while we sang "Solidarity Forever" at the top of our lungs. I would have put up with anything to be a card carrying member of a union, any union.

The euphoria didn't last. Where I lived, full-time jobs for musicians were virtually non-existent; we mostly played part-time, more like hobbyists than professionals. Consequently, our union local had little clout. We never went on strike. We were afraid no one would notice. We couldn't even set up a picket line in front of a non-compliant club. When we tried, marching smartly to and fro, instruments in hand, some passersby thought we were a parade. Others thought we were greeters hired by the management to bring in customers. I didn't get to burn someone in effigy, or anywhere else.

Try as I may, I couldn't win a seat on the executive. The executive consisted mainly of elderly members who had retired from music. They could afford to retire because they exempted themselves from paying dues and received a stipend every time they attended a meeting. That's why I let my name stand. I wanted to retire from trumpet. I didn't run for president, vice-president, or secretary-treasurer. I was prepared to settle for sergeant-at-arms. I had no idea what the sergeant-at-arms was supposed to do. Neither, I suspect, had anyone else. That was all right with me. I would have written my own job description, beginning with burning someone in effigy. But no one took my bid for office seriously. What a disappointment. To pay dues and remain a member, I had to keep blowing that infernal horn.

As ill luck would have it, I couldn't find a unionized job when I finished school. Regretfully, I bade farewell to organized labour and entered the ranks of disorganized labour, never to escape. But I still envy the unions and rejoice in their triumphs. I still admire their work ethic.

Union people work hard. They work hard at getting jobs, especially full-time jobs. They work harder at getting them than at doing them. Once they get them, they work even harder at negotiating fewer hours and more days off. This creates openings for the unemployed. Isn't that considerate of the unions? If they keep it up, the day will come when everyone has a job and no one goes to work. Utopia will have arrived.

But the public-sector unions could spoil the party. They want a four-day work week. Bravo and hats off to them, I say. It's about time they started working four days a week. When bargaining for a new contract, they often tell their members to work to rule. Bravo and Hats off again, I say. That's an improvement I can live with.

Even though I'm no longer a member, I often go to union meetings when the organizers bring in speakers to pump up the troops. It's a real learning experience. Recently, a fiery orator from the East told us that if it weren't for unions, we'd all be working for slave wages. I didn't even know slaves got wages. I always thought they were, well, slaves. But that's the way it is at union meetings. You get pumped up and learn a little history at the same time.

I also learned that unions are among the chief advocates of social programs that redistribute income. These programs keep demand and supply in proper balance and help to ensure that times remain good. When times are good, more people have jobs and many of them work. When times are bad, fewer people have jobs and more people get burned in effigy. I blush to admit it but I'm sometimes tempted to cry, "Let the bad times roll."

Pay no attention to the rumours about union corruption. They're not true. Union bosses don't steal anything they're not entitled to. They never take bribes during working hours. They refuse to lie without a reason. They wouldn't think of bullying their brothers and sisters unless they deserved it, nor would they raid rival unions for members on Sundays or other holy days.

Most of us pay little attention to unions until they go on strike. Striking is what they do best. I especially like strikes that shut down so-called essential services. When we have to do without them, we discover that these services aren't essential at all. Postal service isn't essential and never has been. I recall a postal strike that lasted only half a month. Before it ended, I urged our letter carrier to stay out for the other half. Another two weeks without junk mail, solicitations and bills would have suited me fine. It was like being on vacation. Too bad the telephones couldn't have shut down at the same time.

Our doctors went on strike when the province was introducing medicare. It didn't bother us one bit. We looked after ourselves better than we'd ever done and refused to get sick. That put more pressure on the negotiations than anything the government could have done and the doctors were back at work in no time. But the strike was hard on the pharmacists, who couldn't sell drugs without prescriptions, not to mention the morticians, who couldn't hold funerals without corpses. Much to the relief of both, we started getting sick again as soon as the doctors re-opened their offices.

Once in a very long while, all the unions get together for a general strike. This hasn't happened in my lifetime, but I can always hope. It would be a bit like fasting. They say a fast clears the impurities out of the body. A general strike clears the impurities out of the body politic. Just imagine waking up to the sound of birds, instead of traffic, to the smell of flowers, instead of industrial pollutants, to the sight of visitors, instead of letter carriers, meter readers, pollsters, sales people, building inspectors and garbage collectors. Imagine the thrill of producing your own food, composting the refuse, and getting in touch with your pioneer roots.

Consider the tranquillity of it all. There'd be no bad news, because without radio, television and the press, there'd be no news at all, and everyone knows that no news is good news. Our politicians, bless them, would become invisible. Can you appreciate the sheer relief of not having them harass us daily? I can. Our governments would have nothing to waste our money on. Neither would we. No more shopping. No more eating out. No more commercial entertainment. Without videos and other distractions, we'll learn to talk to each other again. Without gas to put in our cars, we'd learn to walk again.

Everyone could picket and get physically fit because in a general strike no one can keep track of who's in or out of the unions. Best of all, there'd be unlimited opportunities to burn someone in effigy.

Hooked on Golf

THE THING ABOUT GOLFERS is that the truth is not in them. Next to anglers, golfers are the world's most notorious liars.

The deception begins with the image they project. They want you to believe that golf is a sport. It's not. Men can't do sports in plus fours, single breasted coats and neckties. Women can't do sports in billowing skirts and corsets. But that's what they wore when golf first became fashionable. People who play sports get short of breath at least some of the time. The only time golfers get short of breath is when they misfire and have to retrieve a ball caught in the upper branches of a tree.

Golfers want you to believe that they're fit and healthy. They're not. Fitness requires regular exercise. Golfers don't exercise. They golf. Health requires a proper diet. Golfers don't eat properly. They drink improperly in the club house. Every golf club we know of was established as a pretext for drinking to excess. The golf was incidental. That's why the trophy for the British Open is a claret jug. But this is a lie, too. Nowadays, no self-respecting golfer limits himself to claret.

Some golfers falsify their score cards all of the time. All golfers falsify their score cards some of the time. This is the first rule of golf. The other rules have to do with minor details like how to design the courses and play the game.

I choose the word "game" guardedly, because we don't know for sure that it is one. The only thing we know for sure is that it's an addiction. It's the only addiction I know of that parents eagerly turn their children onto. Few fathers and mothers introduce their children to cigarettes or cocaine. Millions introduce them to golf. It reminds me of the stories we used to hear about fathers whose idea of sex education was to take their sons to a prostitute. I don't mean to suggest that golf is as bad as prostitution. I mean to suggest that it's worse. Nobody wastes four hours a day, five or six days a week in a brothel. Lots of people do on a golf course.

Golfers are such prevaricators they can't even agree on the history of what they do. Some say golf began in the Roman Empire. If so, it was probably responsible for the decline and fall of that remarkable institution. Others blame the Dutch, still others the French. Whatever the truth of these allegations, the Scots stand convicted of the modern version of golf and may have lost their independence because of it.

In the mid-fifteenth century, King James II tried unsuccessfully to ban the alleged sport after the flower of Scottish youth took it up in preference to archery, jousting and other martial arts. The King was concerned about military preparedness, and prophetically so. Just over fifty years later, the Scots suffered a merciless defeat at the hands of the English in the Battle of Flodden Field. A golf club can be a wicked weapon and a well hit ball can do a lot of damage to the head, even to the head of an Englishman. But the Scottish golfers were no match for the English archers. The bows and arrows easily won the day.

Golf as we know it originated on the wind-swept linksland of the eastern Scottish coast. This area, which links the foreshore to interior farm land, features sand dunes and fine salt-resistant turf. Formed largely by nature, these classic courses gave the Scots a comparative advantage in the development and export of the putative game. From the seaside golf links, it spread to every continent but Antarctica. Penguins, apparently, are immune to golf and, unlike people, they aren't interested in missing links.

I don't play golf either. That's why I can write about it objectively. I choose to abstain because there's no challenge in golf. It might be challenging to drop a square object into a round opening or a round object into a square opening. Where's the challenge in dropping a round object into a round opening, especially when nobody tries to stop you? In basketball, you only have to drop a round object into a round opening, but there are five giants determined to wrestle it away from you. In football, you only have to push an oval object over a straight line, but a couple of tons of living lard have other ideas. In hockey, you only have to direct a flat object into a rectangular cavity, but there are six armed vigilantes trying to knock you over.

Golfers may walk down the fairway together, but they don't obstruct one another. Golf is the athletic equivalent of solitaire. When four golfers get liquored up for eighteen holes, it's like four card players getting soused for an afternoon of one-on-one with a deck. The only obstacles to successful golf are the courses. The architects who design these acreages try to misdirect the players with rolling hills, varied slopes, sparkling lagoons, shimmering sand, emerald groves, and an abundance of small wildlife. The architects know that golfers are easily distracted by glimpses of paradise.

It doesn't take much intelligence to play golf, but it takes a fair amount to quit playing. Golfers are forever getting caught in the rain and struck by lightening. The intelligent ones go home before that happens. I gained some insight into this when I visited the Royal and Ancient Golf Club of St Andrews, where uniform rules for the reputed sport were codified in 1897. St. Andrews, site of one of the first courses in Scotland, is on the North Sea. The wind coming off that frigid expanse is cold enough to numb the brain of even the most warm-blooded players. The condition, apparently, is contagious. That's why golfers find it so absorbing to drop round balls into round holes. That's why they don't know enough to come in out of the rain.

Exit Walking

WHEN I TOOK A CAB recently, the driver spent most of the time complaining about other motorists. I couldn't resist the journalistic urge to ask who, in his opinion, are the worst drivers.

"Old guys like you," he replied.

I like frankness in cab drivers even when they're only half right.

"It's true," I said, "that traffic accident rates are highest among the elderly, but not among old guys like me. I don't drive. I've never owned a car."

"Do you have a family?" he asked

"My children are grown up."

"Are they in counselling?"

"What on earth for?"

"To help them adjust to a mobile society. You're lucky if they're not suing you?"

"On what grounds?"

"Negligence, failure to provide necessities, cruel and unusual punishment — ."

"Surely you don't consider a car a necessity."

"Maybe not when you were growing up, Grandpa," he said, accusingly, "but in case you haven't noticed, there's been an automotive revolution over the last fifty years. The basic necessities are food, clothing, shelter and wheels, though not necessarily in that order."

I was beginning to wonder whether he might not be right. Every household in my neighbourhood had not just one car but several. It was that way all over town. Despite the example I set them, even my children had cars.

"All my kids drive," I told him. "They started as soon as the law allowed, if not sooner. My pedestrian lifestyle hasn't held them back."

"Your wife must drive then."

"She's a pedestrian, too. Neither of us has ever owned or rented a car."

"You people are subversives," he said, shaking his head gravely. "If everyone was like you the economy would collapse and we'd be in political turmoil."

"Perhaps," I replied, "but think what a boon it would be for cab drivers like you."

While he pondered this, I assured him that cars show no signs of declining in popularity. On the contrary, our passion for driving seems limitless. Pedestrians, on the other hand, are an endangered species, practically on the edge of extinction. Each time I venture out, I get the impression that certain motorists are intent on pushing us over the edge.

When I exited the cab, he was still shaking his head and I couldn't stop musing on the automotive revolution he had drawn to my attention. I still can't. I recall how the objectives of the auto makers have expanded from a car for every home, to two cars for every home, to a car for every individual, to a car for every pursuit — a convertible for dating, a sports utility vehicle for hunting, a van for family driving, a sedan for employment, a half-ton truck for garage sales and auctions. I don't know where it will end, but when I reflect on the refusal of some celebrities to wear the same outfit twice, I see that the auto makers have a way to go and we seem willing to follow.

While the human birth rate has been below replacement level for decades, the vehicular production rate is exploding. Given a choice between another child and another car, most motorists opt for the vehicle. They consider driving a right. It's way up there with the right to life. As a matter of fact, it takes precedence over the right to life. Compared to people, relatively few cars are rejected on the assembly line.

I'm surprised the cab driver didn't ask me how I get around. Everyone asks me how I get around. First, though, most give me the benefit of the doubt. They assume, merely because I'm out and about, that I'm a motorist like them. "What are you driving these days?" they'll ask, just to make conversation. Or, "Did you leave your car in lot B?" Or, "Can I give you a lift to your vehicle?" No matter how often I hear it, the last question astonishes me. I can't easily process the idea that I need the services of two cars, one of which I use to get to the other.

When the startling truth that I don't drive can no longer be avoided, even perfect strangers want to know how I get around. Well, I tell them, I walk around, bus around, cab around, fly around and sail around. I've also been known to skate around, ski around, bike around and horse around. Although a quite private person, I'm not embarrassed to be seen walking in public or using public transport.

Legs, unaided by natural or artificial conveniences, are my chief method of locomotion. Since taking my first step, I've walked tens of thousands of miles without having to trade them in. Never have they broken down, required repairs, or been subject to recall to furnish missing parts. I've seen legs that are prettier than mine, but none more serviceable.

When I don't feel like talking about my unusual life style, I sometimes pass as a motorist. It's easy for a pedestrian to pass as a motorist. I slouch along, feign shortness of breath, lean on things and fiddle with my house keys. If that seems less than convincing, I indulge in some simulated road rage, shouting at aggressive motorists from the cross walk and clenching my fists. I draw the line, though, at reaching for a non-existent weapon.

It doesn't bother me that I've never owned a car. On the contrary, I'm delighted that a car has never owned me. Eventually, all motorists reach a stage or an age when they have to bid their cars farewell and learn to walk all over again. Withdrawal from driving is so traumatic that many motorists never fully recover. Withdrawal is something non-drivers like me don't have to cope with. Given a little luck, we walk 'til we drop.

Safaris in Suburbia

THE THEORY that men and women are alike breaks down in the supermarket. Women shoppers know where everything is. They just have to go out and collect it. Women are gatherers. Men shoppers don't know where anything is. They have to look for it. Men are hunters.

For women, grocery shopping is a chore. For men, it's an adventure. That's why you see so many retired men pushing shopping carts. After a lifetime of sober industry, they've rediscovered the joy of the hunt. Any day of the week, up one aisle and down the other, you can observe them stalking their prey, while their wives quietly stock up.

Why, you might ask, don't they get a floor plan and become gatherers? Well, that makes about as much sense as asking why trappers don't become fur farmers or why fishermen don't go in for aquaculture. They're responding to a primeval passion. I know, because every time I get hold of a shopping cart it happens to me. I feel a spurt of adrenaline and can't wait to start tracking the groceries.

The managers know what we're up to and thwart us at every turn. It begins with the signage over the aisles. These signs aren't just vague. They're misleading. Take the ones that say canned vegetables and fruit, for instance. No self-respecting male goes hunting for a can of vegetables or fruit. He's looking for diced carrots, cut green beans, or creamed corn. He wants crushed pineapple or squashed apricots. But the tins are so cleverly concealed under a protective cover of confusing brand names and garish labels that he's tempted to throw up his hands and go after the fresh produce.

If he perseveres, he discovers that there are no refried beans. Refried beans may come in cans, but the other beans want nothing to do with them. So he has to ask the nearest female shopper, who sends him wheeling off to the ethnic section. Sure enough, there are the refried beans, along with a variety of other ethnic products whose names he can't pronounce. But where are the Polish sausages, the Jap oranges, the Danish pastries? Where's the French toast? The supermarkets, he finds, are not above discriminating on the basis of ethnic origin.

He discovers the Polish sausages hiding out with the Canadian bacon and the Jap oranges snuggling up against the Spanish onions. The Danish pastries are off cavorting with the English muffins in a bakery section that includes French bread, but no toast. By the time he sorts it out, he's ready for an Irish coffee.

Then it's off to the canned meat and seafood and he's in trouble again. He's not looking for meat. He wants flaked turkey, chopped liver or bruised ham. He's not interested in seafood. He wants smoked oysters, broken shrimp or mutilated crab. He's after snails but all he can see is escargot. The managers are playing with him again. Defeated, he recoils from the thought of canned food and settles for the fresh variety.

But he has to be a butcher or a biologist to track the different cuts of meat. He can tell a rump roast from a rib roast without the help of labels, but try as he may he can't find a pot roast. The exotic types of cattle they bring in nowadays probably don't have pots. The geneticists have bred the pots right out of them.

He flees to the fresh fruits and vegetables and here, indeed, he finds a happy hunting ground. There's no deceptive packaging, no attempt at camouflage. What you see is what you get. Well, almost. If he's not careful, he's liable to bag plantains instead of bananas, bok choy instead of celery, or persimmons instead of tomatoes. Eggplants can be confusing, too. They look as if they belong with the organ meats.

As every woman knows, the last stop on any shopping trip is the frozen-food section. Once again, he encounters discrimination, not on the basis of ethnicity, but of class. Since the packaged products are usually more refined than the unpackaged, they tend to hang out together. So he shouldn't expect to see a package of frozen breaded codfish consorting with a codfish frozen whole. It just isn't done, certainly not in the better supermarkets. Nor should he expect to see the frozen foods associating with the previously frozen. The previously frozen are meat or fish that have thawed out voluntarily. They've lost status and may not be frozen again.

When he arrives at the check-out line, he's exhausted but triumphant. He has re-validated his primal role and re-charged his self-esteem. Despite the frustrations, he's already thinking about the next outing and is determined to do better. He notices that the women shoppers don't share his enthusiasm. They're relieved that the trip is nearly over and are content to scan the tabloids. That's another difference between them. The women like to eye the tabloids. The men like to eye the women.

Commercial Art

I NOTICE from the television commercials that child labour is back in fashion. Not only commercials that target the young, like the ones promoting breakfast food or its facsimile, but those aimed primarily at adults are increasingly employing children, including toddlers and infants.

Some of these vignettes are quite explicit. A couple I regularly see entail partial nudity, intimate contact and simulated passion. They portray adult care-givers who wipe, diaper, stroke and caress underage co-stars without obtaining their informed consent. When these tots grow up, they could sue the sponsors. Don't be surprised if they seek damages for being commercially exploited, sexually compromised and publicly humiliated. I hope they don't sue the viewers.

I've also noticed a commercial about a little girl who bursts out of her bathroom in some disarray and sets off in search of a roll of the sponsor's toilet paper. I imagine the producer got a child to do it because no adult actress wanted to be seen traipsing through the house with her panties around her ankles.

Compared to other art forms, the TV commercial is in its infancy. This, no doubt, is why it is partial to infants and children. I suspect it will undergo a great deal of experimentation before reaching maturity. Since I enjoy the commercials, childish or otherwise, far more than most other TV offerings, I feel honoured to be a witness to their creative evolution. The TV people know this and often show me eight or ten commercials without the interruption of a single program.

I especially enjoy the plots. They're usually more varied and complex than those of the programs that intervene. The standard program opens with a problem and proceeds to the solution, but not directly. Almost invariably there is a brief interlude during which it looks as if the solution might not materialize.

In commercial art this is known as the What-will-I-do-now? plot. The leading character suffers from dirty linen, rough hands, itchy feet, or nosey neighbours, all or any of which are likely to produce unpleasant consequences. These are averted only by the timely application of the advertised detergent, lotion, fungicide, or pepper spray.

The reverse of this is the My-life-will-never-be-the-same-now-that-I've-discovered-it plot. It opens dramatically with the solution, after which the problem that needed solving is revealed. In this, the protagonist caresses a bottle of cooking oil, a jar of dental adhesive, or a can of insecticide; and the narrator, by skillful repetition of the phrase, "No more clogged arteries, wobbly dentures, or lousy hair" conjures up the seriousness of the problem, which happily has ceased to exist.

Either of these plots may be embellished with a problem twist, an unexpected turn of events that is both satisfying and tantalizing. Specifically, the solution to one problem creates another, which neither the actors nor the viewers wish ever to see solved. It is best illustrated by the college man who, spurned by women because of his rough beard, switches to the sponsor's subcutaneous razor, and faces the entirely new problem of how to cope with the gaggle of female admirers who insist on dancing with him cheek to cheek.

Commercials often invite public participation, something most programs rarely do. In its most elementary form, participation is secured by requesting the viewers to "try it and see for yourself." At a more advanced level, innocent bystanders are asked to decide such weighty questions as which hair is the greasiest or which teeth the yellowest, all without benefit of script or rehearsal.

The superiority of commercials over programs is due partly to their greater freedom in borrowing techniques from the past. The Shakespearean soliloquy is a common one, used to excellent effect in a commercial about an eight-year-old boy rejoicing over a set of animal cards. During a pause in the action, his mother turns to the viewers and says: "Johnny just loves his new picture cards, and we (nodding to her husband and holding up a rectangular package) just love the pound of tea that is included at no extra cost."

Less common, but equally effective, are commercials that revive the chorus from ancient Greece. Nothing I know of can surpass the earthy boldness of a bevy of breathtaking beauties flaunting their ample hair while the chorus admonishes: "Don't settle for shampoo. Insist on Realpoo."

Some commercials, though self-contained, are also segments of a continuing saga. Two youngsters in a supermarket reach for the same box of cereal, and from one episode to the next their friendship grows along with their appetite for Flaky Flax. Or, a fetching woman and her charming neighbour reveal a common addiction to the same brand of iced tea and find themselves in a romantic relationship that blossoms through an eight-part commercial mini-series with extensive re-runs.

The more successful commercials are re-run daily, hourly, half-hourly or more often, month after month. No mere program has that kind of staying power. As a result of it, we can't avoid identifying commercial performers with the roles they play: whenever we see the woman in the Drain-Flo commercial, she's pouring her sponsor's solvent into the sink; whenever we see the man in the Porterhouse Coffee commercial, he's drinking his sponsor's beverage.

Although a stable cast ensures familiarity and predictability, contracts eventually expire and performers change roles. This can be upsetting if, without warning, we see the Drain-Flo woman drinking her product and the Porterhouse Coffee man pouring his into the sink.

Like all true art, TV commercials are culturally revealing. Two thousand years hence, the discovery of a cache of commercials will tell far more about us than the Rosetta stone or the Dead Sea Scrolls told about our predecessors. If nothing else survives, the TV spots will give future archeologists and historians a pretty good idea how we lived and why we died out.

I can imagine a group of them scanning the commercials for fast food and declaring: "No wonder those dim witted *Homo sapiens* went into decline. They had to be reminded to eat." Or another group discovering that whatever the commercials touted, most of them were sexually suggestive, and exclaiming: "No wonder those weak willed *Homo sapiens* are extinct. They had to be prompted to mate."

Looking Back

IS THERE SOMETHING WRONG with me? I don't remember where I was or what I was doing when I heard about President Kennedy's assassination back in 19 . . . uh, back in the sixties. It's the same with Paul Henderson's winning goal when the Canadians beat the Russians in international hockey back in . . . uh, sometime later.

The pundits say that since these are defining events in our common life, we ought to remember the context in which we experienced them. There are all sorts of defining events, I suppose, not the least of which may be the blessed events that mark our entry into the world. But I don't remember the context of even my own birth, let alone of hockey's re-birth or Kennedy's death. I suspect I was with my mother and I imagine she was with me. But that's only hearsay. I have no memory of it.

I don't know what these highly touted events are supposed to define. I don't even know what makes them defining. Maybe being first is what counts. Certainly, it was the first time the NHL beat the Russians and I suspect it was the first time President Kennedy was assassinated. Apart from that, the criteria seem rather vague.

Getting my first dog may have been a defining event for me. The context is as clear now as it was then. Tiny was a politically correct puppy, inter-racial and multicultural. That was before we'd even heard of political correctness.

So on good days we called him a mongrel, on bad days a mutt. In spite of his mixed heritage, or because of it, he was a smart dog. As soon as he entered our home, he marked his territory.

My mother took over his training. Whenever he wet the floor, she would stick his nose in it and put him outside. I thought it was kind of cruel. But mom knew what she was doing and Tiny was a quick study. In no time at all he learned that if he wanted outside, he had to wet the floor.

Another possibly defining event was my first romantic kiss. I had recently entered Grade seven and a girl I couldn't take my eyes off of let me walk her home from an evening skating party. Not wanting to be observed, I directed her down the unlighted alley behind her house. There, knee-deep in snow, I kissed her firmly on the cheek, somewhere between her nose and her garbage can. I remember everything about that magic, star-filled night and how I demonstrated my undying affection for . . . uh, her name's in the school yearbook, I imagine.

I suppose my first paying job was something of a defining event, too. Following Grade eight, I worked nine hours a day, six days a week at a local service station and garage. The pay, five dollars a week, shocked my friends. Even in those benighted times, they thought I was being exploited. I didn't think so. I had nothing better to do for the summer and it was five dollars a week I wouldn't otherwise have owned. Besides, I was learning how to fix cars and swear.

It was certainly a defining event when I went bald for the first time. If nothing else, it defined my hairline. To cope with it, I made common cause with other differently follicled people and we founded a support group to defend the rights of the non-hirsute community. When I put together a band to play dances and other social gatherings, I insisted on being an equal-opportunity employer. Consequently, at no time did the number of hairless musicians fall below their proportion in the general population. I was very proud of that bit of affirmative action and I can't understand why the band never went anywhere.

But events like a first dog, a first kiss, a first job or a first traumatic hair loss are personal. The pundits are thinking communally. The declaration of war in 1939 should satisfy them. If anything qualifies as a communal defining event, that surely does. It wasn't the first world war, but it was my first world war. I'll never forget waking up to shouts of "Extra! Extra! War Blazes in Poland" from a newsboy in the street. In some obscure way, he may have defined my future, Eventually, I became a reporter and learned how to dig up news. Then I went into public relations and learned how to cover it up.

Too young to fight, I followed the war on the radio, bought victory bonds, collected scrap metal to be turned into weapons and revelled in the mock air raids and phony blackouts that were staged to test our vigilance. I saw every war picture Hollywood put out and loved them all, especially the musicals with their big bands and beautiful girls. In the movies and in real life, beautiful girls seemed to be always saying goodbye to their boyfriends in uniform. The war was still on when I turned sixteen and, patriot that I was, I vowed to do something about those sad farewells. As an added contribution to the war effort, I dated as many lonely beauties as I could find and helped them forget the boys they promised to remember. As they say, war is hell.

Maybe we remember only what we want to. Maybe as recent memory fades with age or infirmity, distant memory grows more creative. Did I really date those wartime beauties or was it wishful fantasy? Several of the old musicals are available on videotape. The bands are as big and the girls as beautiful as ever. I haven't fared quite as well. Still, I enjoy those old movies with their young girls and puerile plot lines. They take me back to a time when reality and fantasy often merged and no one seemed to care. So why should I care now?

Getting defined as a reporter was psychologically bracing. It allowed me to re-define reality for anyone who heard or read my stuff. In those days, we didn't backstop our note taking with tape recorders — they were too large and heavy to lug around — and few, if any, of us knew shorthand. This made for some pretty creative reporting. I specialized in local politics, what we called the city hall beat. I discovered early on that local politicians hated being misquoted. The only thing they hated more was being quoted accurately. They expected us to clean up the grammar, make clear what was vague, and eliminate the profanity. They were all news junkies. They could hardly wait to find out what they'd said.

Part of my job as a public relations flak was to translate academic jargon into the *lingua franca* of journalism. This enabled me to sanitize the news before the reporters got hold of it. One incident in particular stands out. My university bosses were fretting over a policy statement that embodied a proposal to revise the objectives and senior job descriptions of a department that dealt extensively with the public. The board of governors had already approved the statement and the departmental brass wanted to get the word out. But the writing was so vague and convoluted no one could understand it. When summoned, even the authors failed to enlighten the president and his aides. After a frustrating exchange, the meeting broke up and one of the vice-presidents called me over.

"Here," he said, as he handed me a copy of the statement, "make this say something."

I couldn't understand it either. But this had never stopped me before. I drafted a news release detailing what I thought the statement ought to say and circulated it for approval. Nobody changed a word and everyone seemed relieved. The authors seemed especially pleased when they discovered the precise nature of their departmental aims and duties.

Later that year, my creative news release was recognized at the national convention of university public relations flaks. One flak's idea of entertainment was to form a choir of delegates and render university news releases in Gregorian chant. Mine was the first on his program. Now there's a defining event for you.

School's Out

IF YOU LIKE WATCHING grass grow, you'll love seeing students graduate. Graduation ceremonies are so repetitious and predictable, you can't help longing for a parading student to trip on a gown or a sleeping dignitary to fall out of a chair. Since neither is likely to happen, the only refuge from relentless boredom is a fertile imagination. Sometimes I imagine that I'm judging livestock and assigning points for grooming, structural integrity, muscling, and rump fat. Other times I imagine that I'm witnessing a mass execution at which the official charged with hooding the students strangles them.

My imagination is particularly active during university graduations, more than a hundred of which I endured at close quarters as a media relations flak for my *alma mater.* *Alma mater*, which is Latin for nourishing or fostering mother, is a misnomer. There is little that is nourishing or fostering about an institution that repeatedly inflicts graduation exercises on faculty, students, administrators and innocent members of the public. The only other Latin expression I remember from those tedious events is *in absentia,* a condition I devoutly wished had applied to me.

Although I have left the university, I have not escaped graduations. No one with relatives or friends escapes graduations. You would think that other institutions might have avoided the worst features of the university exercises. They have not avoided them. They have built on them. All graduations are the same graduation, from kindergarten up or, depending on your perspective, down. I wonder how many times I can listen to "Pomp and Circumstance" and remain civil. Not many more, I suspect.

The only graduation I fondly recall was my own, and it isn't because I was named, hooded, presented with a diploma and photographed in drag, although these interruptions relieved the monotony somewhat. No, it's because a woman with enormous platform shoes tripped while ascending to the stage, and promptly descended; and, more important, one of the dignitaries, hoary with age and creeping senility, slept through three-quarters of the ceremony. He didn't fall out of his chair, but he did the next best thing. He wet his pants. This provided sufficient food for thought and fodder for whispered conversation to give respite to the weary spectators close enough to the stage to notice.

Diversions like that are rare, unfortunately, which is why I attend graduations under protest. It would be tiresome enough if I just had to watch hundreds of students march, plod, slouch or shuffle their way to the diplomas. But I don't just have to watch graduands who turn into graduates. I have to listen to speakers who turn into hypnotists. If you suffer from insomnia, take in a couple of graduations and call me in the morning.

Often the main speakers are survivors of earlier graduations. One speaker I was subjected to compounded my boredom by describing her own ceremony in numbing detail and announcing that it was the first step in a challenging journey that culminated in the graduation she was now prolonging. Then, prolonging it further, she described the journey, after which she gave the comatose students the benefit of her advice. These speakers nearly always give advice, whether they are addressing graduates from kindergarten, elementary school, high school, university or any number of other post-secondary institutions whose administrators think they gain credibility by adopting rituals that have afflicted us since the middle ages.

Sometimes the main speakers are world leaders in their fields. Seldom are they world leaders in the art of giving interesting speeches. One speaker I endured at a ceremony that started in the morning rambled on into the afternoon. He made matters worse by announcing half way through that he hadn't come all this distance to give a short speech.

A high school graduation I felt obliged to attend featured two valedictorians, one of each sex, who were vying for the honour of making the most grammatical errors in a single paragraph. Valedictorians are supposed to be the best students. I hoped fervently that in this instance they were not. I wanted to believe that their selection was a concession to political correctness, not a reflection of academic performance.

Fortunately, they faced a temperamental microphone and I didn't hear all that they had to say. The teacher who followed dispensed with the microphone and projected his voice like a trained orator. I had no difficulty hearing his grammatical errors.

Why, you might wonder, do we persevere in droves through one or more punishing graduations every year? Well, a few of us are reporters and we feel that we ought to be there in case something happens. The rest of us have been invited by parents, children, grandchildren, siblings, spouses, other relatives, or friends who are graduating, and we feel that we ought to show up to offer them moral support. Otherwise, they might not go through with it.

I see no relief ahead. Just about everyone seems to be graduating from something. A lucky few are able to graduate *in absentia*. Maybe I can learn how to attend *in absentia*.

All the Way to the Bank

THE LAST TIME I made a deposit at the bank I asked the teller for three pounds of bananas.

"I beg your pardon," she said.

"Three pounds of bananas, please," I repeated.

"Are you sure you're not bananas?"

Tellers aren't usually that rude. When I told her so, she called the manager. They conferred briefly and without further inquiry he took the teller's side.

"Yes, we have no bananas," he said. "Why would you think otherwise?"

"I assumed that you'd carry bananas," I explained, "because one of the supermarkets I patronize offers banking services."

I was feeling expansive that day and decided to give them another chance.

"If you want to change your story," I added, "I don't mind bagging the bananas myself."

They refused to back down. I had no choice but to get my bananas at the supermarket. In retaliation, I opened a small account there. That ought to teach the teller and her snooty manager a lesson.

Banks could learn a lot about merchandising from supermarkets. At least once a month staff at the more trendy stores prepare tidbits of barbecued beef, spiced ham, curried chicken, apple strudel, you name it, and invite customers to sample them. When has a bank teller invited you to sample a dime or try a quarter? To move products at the end of their shelf life, supermarket managers often reduce the price for quick sale. When has a bank manager reduced the price of a worn out silver dollar or offered a deal on a tattered C-note?

Supermarkets truck some of their aging perishable goods to food depots to feed the hungry. When have banks trucked some of their old currency to shelters to support the homeless? Never, in my experience. They send it to the central bank to be shredded. Enterprising supermarkets develop their own product lines with distinctive brand names. I've yet to come across any banks enterprising enough to print or mint their own cash.

They weren't always so lacking in initiative. Long before the supermarkets thought of stocking ethnic foods, the banks introduced foreign currencies. It was a brilliant merchandizing coup, but instead of building on it, the top executives got sidetracked into automating and computerizing everything in sight, including some of the tellers. Now you can do your banking unsullied by human contact.

Progressive supermarkets have posted welcomers at the entrance to greet customers. When have you been greeted at the entrance of a bank? The supermarkets also set up customer service desks. With few questions asked, the clerks give you speedy refunds on goods that fail to perform as intended. When has a banker given you a refund on an investment loan that failed to perform as intended?

No wonder banks have an image problem. They're perceived as unimaginative, insensitive and parsimonious.

They're also seen as dull, unfeeling and stingy. Even robbers have noticed it. That's why they prey on banks but rarely target supermarkets. The term bank robber has become entrenched in the language. There's no evidence that supermarket robber is going to be similarly honoured. Have you noticed that bank robbers nearly always wear masks? They're ashamed to be recognized in places like that.

Banks lend out the money which depositors like you and me put into our accounts. Not only do they lend the money they have. Through overdrafts, they lend money they don't have. This is one advantage they've managed to retain and develop. So far, the supermarkets haven't figured out how to sell goods they don't have.

I don't know how the banks get away with it. If you or I tried it we'd go to jail. The police look askance at people who make deals with money they don't have. They look the other way when the banks do it.

In days gone by, these lending practices made banks wildly popular. Periodically, depositors would rush in en masse to withdraw their cash. They called this quaint custom a run on the bank. Supermarkets were never that sought after. Even today, customers don't rush into supermarkets en masse to empty the shelves.

To say that banks are no longer wildly popular would be an understatement. Nowadays, they're so out of favour many depositors refuse to walk into them, let alone run. If anything, they run the other way. They abandon their accounts and go into hiding. For the banks, it's a public relations disaster. They're embarrassed about having all that unclaimed money to lend. They prefer lending money they don't have.

I wouldn't want to say anything to undermine faith in the banking system. Without faith it wouldn't work. It's important that depositors believe they can take out all their cash whenever they want to. It doesn't help them to know that if they all wanted to take it out at the same time there wouldn't be enough to go around. So I'm not going to tell them.

Breakfast in Bed

ONCE, WHEN I WAS YOUNG AND RECKLESS, I decided to surprise my wife with breakfast in bed. Even in those benighted times, husbands were known to cook and the outcome was often surprising. I don't remember what motivated me. I suspect it may have been her birthday. I know it wasn't Mother's Day. On Mother's Day I expected her to surprise me with breakfast in bed. That's the day women are supposed to act like ideal wives and mothers. On this day, I was determined to act like an ideal husband and father.

Getting her breakfast was one thing. I felt reasonably capable of preparing and delivering a light meal. Surprising her was something else. With four pre-schoolers under foot, I felt threatened with exposure at every turn. Later, when the four became nine, my wife was lucky to get breakfast at all, let alone in bed.

I began my preparations sometime after eleven o'clock the night before. I would have started earlier, but I had to wait until she was asleep. One by one I carried the slumbering children from their beds upstairs to the living room below, where I deposited the three eldest in make-shift arrangements on the floor and the baby in a perambulator in the hall. When they awoke in the morning, rubbing their eyes incredulously, as children do, delighted and apparently astonished at being alive, and shouting, screaming, kicking, and tearing in sheer exultation, my wife would sleep on. It was delicate and painstaking work, which I finished sometime after midnight.

By one o'clock I had set the table for the children's breakfast, putting out oranges, which had only to be cut into wedges, toast, which had only to be re-heated and buttered, and cereal, which had only to be soaked in milk and sprinkled with sugar. With everything about ready when the children awoke, their attention would be diverted from weakening the foundations of the house to strengthening the foundations of their little bodies, while I stole quietly upstairs to rouse my sleeping wife and confront her with breakfast.

Timing was vital. The rousing and confronting would have to be completed before the meal downstairs was demolished so that I would be there to channel the dear ones into the open, where they could harmlessly pull up a lawn or break down a tree. All would be lost, my wife's breakfast included, if they got into our bedroom.

I had a pot of coffee percolating by one-fifteen. I needed it to keep alert and would be able to re-heat what was left later in the morning, thereby saving time when every second counted. I put my wife's ham in the frying pan, the eggs in a bowl on the stove beside it, two slices of bread in the toaster, a glass of orange juice in the fridge and, in the event that the elaborate scheme came apart, a bottle of gin in the stairway.

With everything in order, I reckoned that I would be able to prepare her meal in less than ten minutes. If I could have relied on getting it done before the children awoke, all would be well. But this was too much to expect. To distract them for a few minutes between waking and eating, I called in the help of their favourite playthings.

The mechanical dog that walked on two legs (It had no choice as they had torn off the other two within minutes of getting it) I placed looking out coyly from the ceiling lamp. They would enjoy that, and their vain attempts to scale the walls to dislodge it would consume two minutes at least. Some of their other animal toys, like the headless giraffe, the trunkless elephant, the horseless rider, and the catless tail, I placed behind the furnace registers, so that they looked as if they were in cages. The children would see the point immediately, the suggestion that the toys were behind bars for their own protection. I made pyramids with the different-sized containers they had collected, and buildings and bridges with their wooden blocks. It takes only a few seconds to knock down structures like that, but in this venture a few seconds could be the difference between success and failure. I hung their cars and trucks on clothes hooks in the hall; and the clothes they were to wear, I laid out to form on the living room floor, like children in a two-dimensional world.

It was after two when I finished, feeling rather weary, but also very superior and cunning. To deceive your wife in such a matter would be quite an accomplishment; to fool your children as well was almost unheard of. Leaving a couple of bottles ready should the baby stir in what was left of the morning, I rehearsed the plan mentally from beginning to end and retired upstairs. To avoid disturbing my wife, I settled in the spare room; but first, I removed the alarm clock from the head of her bed and set it for six-thirty at the head of mine. That was half an hour earlier than the children were in the habit of descending on us. In a few minutes I was asleep.

I awoke without help from the alarm, feeling surprisingly rested and eager to bound into action. It was a bright, cheery morning. Sitting up in bed I became conscious of the familiar sounds of the street: trucks passing over the road in front, causing the house to vibrate, and some of the neighbourhood children, many of whom rose before six, chipping pieces out of the sidewalk, with the same effect.

I could almost smell the delicious breakfast I was about to cook. Turning to the door, I saw it.

"Here," my wife said, frowning as she handed me ham and eggs still sizzling on the plate, "I took the hint."

I looked at the clock: nine-thirty AM.

The Irish Connection

MY IMMIGRANT MOTHER once told me that she had booked passage for America on the *Titanic*. For some reason I can't recall, she changed to another ship. That was the first time I'd heard of the *Titanic* and its fatal rendezvous with an iceberg. Although dutifully thankful, I soon forgot the incident. Indeed, I might not have given it a second thought if the world hadn't become obsessed with the ill-fated luxury liner and disasters in general.

It seems that every other person I meet knows of someone who planned to board the *Titanic*, but didn't. It's a good thing they didn't. If all of them did, the ship would have sunk before leaving the harbour. I wonder what kind of movie that would have made.

I don't understand this fascination with the *Titanic*. I'm more interested in the iceberg. The iceberg was the winner, the *Titanic* the loser. Why do so many people identify with the loser? Salvage crews risked lives and money locating the *Titanic* under tons of water and sand. As far as I know, not a single crew has tried to locate the iceberg fully exposed on the surface. It could be floating around unmelted to this day with evidence of the fateful collision imbedded in it, but no one seems interested enough to mount a search.

When people aren't obsessed with the sinking of the *Titanic*, they're focused on the raising of it. They can't seem to get enough of that unseaworthy vessel. Memorabilia from the *Titanic* are showing up everywhere. There's enough of it, as they say, to sink a ship. They've made a fuss over telegrams from the *Titanic*, life preservers from the *Titanic*, jewelry from the *Titanic*, money from the *Titanic*, furniture from the *Titanic*, booze from the *Titanic*, garbage from the *Titanic*, jokes from the *Titanic* — there's no end to it. It's like an international scavenger hunt. Aficionados are actually seeking out the graves of passengers whose bodies were recovered from the *Titanic*. I don't know what they do when they find them. I'd rather not think about it.

People you'd least suspect seem intent on establishing a link with the *Titanic*. Maybe they expect an apology and compensation for everyone touched by it, however remotely. Maybe they're looking for an affirmative action program. I could get in on that. Since my mother narrowly escaped taking the doomed vessel, I consider myself a *Titanic* survivor. I might be due for a big payoff.

Stranger things have happened. One of my granddaughters got admitted to a language course restricted to francophones after we discovered a French branch on the family tree. We're all now dusting off our resumes. We could be short listed for public relations jobs in Ottawa.

The *Titanic* was built in Belfast, Northern Ireland. If you go there, tour directors will point out the very shipyard. They'll show you the homes the shipbuilders lived in, the pubs they drank at, the streets they fought on, the hospitals they went to, the churches they were buried from. Anyone not building the ship could watch its progress from benches located at a safe distance, and they'll show you the benches. What enthusiasts don't know about the *Titanic* they make up. *Titanic* fiction is almost as popular as *Titanic* fact. It's a titanic boondoggle, that's what it is.

I know very little about the *Titanic*. I went down to our local public library to find out what I could and the computer came up with more than fifty titles. Every one of them was on loan. All I wanted was the cost. I suspect it cost less to build the *Titanic* than it did to shoot the movie. I know that doesn't make sense, but neither does the global fascination with an unsinkable ship that sank.

Would there be that kind of interest if the iceberg had missed its target and the *Titanic* had steamed unharmed into New York harbour? I very much doubt it. We're more interested in the failure of that Irish wonder than the success. It's a revival of an old prejudice against the Irish, of whom I happen to be one, despite the French connection. My parents both grew up around Belfast, in fact.

Those were the days when help wanted signs in New York often specified that no Irish need apply. If the *Titanic* had got through the ice field, I suspect there would have been a sign in the harbour stating: "No Irish ships need apply." Maybe that's why my mother changed vessels.

What a Way to Go

a pre-euro tale

IN PARIS, A YOUNG AMERICAN — I believe she was a student — was photographing the toilets of the restaurant we were dining at. She said she was writing a book on European bathrooms. It was an odd term to use because Europeans don't usually call them bathrooms, not the public ones anyway. In Britain, they often call them loos, on the continent WCs. Everywhere on our tour they also called them toilets, but they didn't always spell or pronounce it that way.

In the hotels we stayed at, bathrooms are what we got. Each had a combination bath and shower, a sink or sometimes two, a toilet and a bidet. At first, I thought the bidet was a toilet in progress and almost used it.

Anyhow, I was glad the American was doing a book. It saved me the trouble. I'd been tempted to do a thesis. It might have earned me a masters degree, even a PhD. I've seen graduate degrees awarded for less weighty research than this.

A fascinating feature of European toilets is the different ways you can flush them. Depending on the model, you can pull a chain, push a button, press or lift a lever, turn a nob, step on a pedal, or do nothing at all and watch the bowl empty automatically; and there are seemingly endless variations of the basic mechanisms. How each works is often not obvious and you can spend a great deal of time figuring them out. It's particularly frustrating when the flush control is separate from the toilet, whether in the ceiling, the wall or the floor. You can't help worrying that you won't find it and will have to ask the attendant for help. The attendant, usually but not always a woman, rarely speaks English. So you pretty well have to show her what it is you're unable to do. They don't mention this in the travel brochures.

One of the principal duties of the attendants is to collect the money. Yes, in most European WCs you pay as you go. It's a barbarous custom, even though it costs only about twenty-five cents a visit in Canadian funds. The problem is that you can't pay in Canadian funds. You require coinage of the country you're relieving yourself in and often you need the exact amount. This is difficult to arrange when you're on tour and changing countries and currencies every few days.

The attendants show no mercy to those who come unprepared. A women on our tour was in some distress when we found the public toilet at Heidelberg Castle. She was a few pfennigs short and couldn't convince the female attendant to let her in. I earned her undying gratitude when I produced a coin that made up the shortfall.

Later, the same woman and I showed up at a toilet that was guarded by a turnstile. To gain admittance, you had to insert a coin that neither of us had, and the ungrateful instrument let in only one customer at a time. Quite a few others shared our predicament and were gesticulating and complaining in several languages. It was like the tower of Babel. I finally crawled under the turnstile and went in without paying. When I returned unscathed, the woman crawled under, too. I averted my eyes out of respect for her feelings because she was much larger than I and must have been a sorry sight.

Public toilets appear to be in short supply in Europe because lineups are frequent, particularly for the women's. I've never been indelicate enough to enquire why. Nor do I complain when in desperation some women refuse to wait any longer and dash into the men's. I rather suspect that in similar circumstances I would do the same.

Some European toilets have no seats and you perch precariously on the rim. Others have no superstructure at all, consisting mainly of a hole in the floor. I thought I'd found one of these uncivilized contraptions in a cubicle in Venice and cursed my luck. But I had been waiting uncomfortably long in a line that was lengthening behind me, and I was in no condition to look for something better. Someone — it turned out to be the male attendant — was rattling the locked cubicle door and holding forth in Italian. He sounded upset, but everyone who speaks animated Italian sounds upset to me, so I kept on with what I was doing. It was only as I turned to leave that I realized a regular toilet had once occupied the cubicle and for whatever reason had been removed. I made a quick getaway, the protests of the attendant ringing in my ears.

Before leaving Italy, I found a WC with a genuine hole-in-the-floor toilet. Since my wife and I arrived together, I gave the attendant, another male, a one-thousand-lire note, about fifty cents, to cover the two of us. It seemed incredible paying a thousand of anything just to answer nature's call. No wonder tourists linger over European toilets and cause painful line-ups. At those prices, no one wants to leave prematurely.

My wife had the hole-in-the-floor model in the women's, together with a sink and running water. I had a regular toilet in the men's, but nothing to wash my hands in. The attendant, who had no English, was singing "O sole mio." This was the first time I'd been serenaded while sitting on the john. It was very moving.

When I came out, I employed sign language to complain about the lack of a wash basin. Still singing, the attendant directed me into the women's, where I was welcomed by a jolly American tourist who had instructed my wife on the safest way to use the floor hole. To put me at ease, the American chatted amiably while I washed my hands and when my wife emerged from her cubicle, I had an opportunity to inspect the skimpy facility.

I don't recall visiting any memorable toilets in Belgium. I do recall that in Brussels they insisted on taking us to a smallish fountain called Manneken Pis. It consists of a little boy with an expression of supreme relief and a bladder that never stops giving. I don't know what all the fuss is about. I saw many a sculptured head with water spewing from the mouth, but as far as I know not one of them has been acclaimed Manneken Puke.

I wouldn't want anyone to think that the toilets were the only highlight of my trip. Buckingham Palace, St. Peter's Basilica, and the Eiffel Tower were also impressive. But they're optional. The toilets are a must.

On with the Show

IT HAPPENS EVERY SUMMER. The fair comes to town and I head for the midway. I've been doing it for as long as I can remember. I'll keep doing it until I can remember no longer. I suspect it has something to do with nostalgia. I reckon I'm trying to recapture the enchantment of visiting the fair as a child. Whenever I entered the midway, it was like Dorothy Gale stepping into the technicolour world of the munchkins from the black and white interior of her Kansas home. Compared to the sights and sounds of the fair, my neighbourhood seemed colourless and muted, too.

Not to mention odourless. There's nothing can match the aroma of a fairground in full cry. The blended fragrance of sizzling hot dogs, fried onions, boiled cabbage, roasted popcorn, spun candy, wet canvas, soggy wood shavings, sweaty grease paint and soft manure evokes more memories than a reunion. One whiff and I'm over the rainbow.

Of course, fairs have changed a lot since I was a boy. For one thing, it's harder to sneak in without paying. For another, some of the acts I liked best are out of favour. I used to make a point of visiting the freaks. Diversity fascinated me, and they were more diverse than the characters in a Dickens novel. Freak shows are no longer socially acceptable. What a pity. The socially proper have succeeded in denying the physically diverse gainful employment. The arbiters of community standards have drummed them out of show business, and as everyone knows, there's no business like show business.

I don't understand it. We're encouraged to watch abnormally thin women modelling clothes on a runway, but not abnormally thin men modelling themselves in a midway. The thin man was one of my favourite freaks. He looked like the stick men I used to draw at school. The first time we met, I offered him food, but he graciously declined. I suspect he didn't want to risk putting on weight in public. The fat lady, often billed as his wife, was also one of my favourites. She rather enjoyed putting on weight in public. It enhanced her marketability. They were great performers. All they had to do was act natural and people flocked to see them. I envied them their easy popularity.

Some of the freaks looked like animals: the dog-faced boy, the elephant man, the cat woman. But that was all right, because some of the animals acted like people: the roller-skating bear, the pirouetting pony, the tight-rope walking tiger. The animal acts are disappearing too. Since I was a boy, animals have acquired rights, except for the right to work at a fair. The socially proper, many of whom keep dogs in a kennel, can't abide seeing seals in a pool. Leave them at sea, they say, where the whales and the polar bears can eat them alive. It's nature's way.

Even without the attentions of the socially proper, freak shows could not have survived, I'm afraid. Few of us will pay to see freaks in a midway when we can see them for nothing all over town. I'm not just talking about the anorexic and the obese. I'm talking about the body builders, male and female, who pump iron and inject steroids until their muscles bulge like sausages. I'm talking about spiked hairdos every colour of the rainbow, full-body tattoos that look like graffiti in motion, pierced ears, noses, tongues, navels and any other body parts well enough defined to put rings through, backs scarred by branding, breasts bursting with silicone, and nails painted like bruises. I'm talking about freaks who are made not born.

I also miss the midgets. As a pre-adolescent, I couldn't get enough of their musical revues and watched them over and over again. There was always a pert little girl — actually, she was a woman at least three times my age — singing "Sweet Leilani" or some other romantic standard. I was smitten before the end of the first chorus. It was puppy love at first sight. Of course, I bore my unrequited feelings silently, realizing that nothing could come of them, and when she left town with the fair, I sometimes grieved for half an hour.

Most fairgoers considered the midgets freaks because they were abnormally small. I wonder if the midgets didn't consider us freaks, because we were abnormally large. I suspect that if we were in the minority instead of them, they'd call us giants, and justifiably so. Maybe they don't suffer from too little growth hormone. Maybe we suffer from too much. Who's to say? Instead of trying to make them bigger, maybe we should be trying to make us smaller. If we did, maybe it would make the environment last longer.

The midgets, the freaks and the animals may be gone or going, but the magicians, the hypnotists, the ventriloquists, the acrobats, the contortionists, the jugglers and the clowns are still allowed. This is live entertainment at its best, and worst. There are no replays when the performers soar, no re-takes when they crash. Nothing ever happens quite the same way twice. I've got a soft spot in my heart for the clowns. Even at their funniest, they're irrepressibly melancholy. I've got a soft spot in my head for the magicians. They fool me every time.

I no longer toss baseballs at milk bottles or throw darts at balloons in a futile bid for a stuffed panda bear. I gave that up in my middle teens, after discovering that no amount of practice could increase my chances of winning. More fascinating than the skill-testing games was the mind-bending patter of the barkers who ran them. They could spot a sucker at a glance and fleece him within minutes. I know because I often watched them do it — to me. I still like to watch and listen, but from a safe distance.

I also watch the rides from a safe distance. I admire fairgoers who enjoy being whirled, shaken, stretched, tossed, squeezed, and accelerated all at the same time. I can't even manage the merry-go-round without feeling queazy. It wasn't always that way. I remember when I'd stuff myself with a loaded hot dog, candy floss and ice cream, do a turn on the roller coaster and get off famished. But there comes a time in everyone's life when it's best not to do the rides on a full stomach. Identifying the time can be difficult. That's why I watch from a safe distance.

Once during the untroubled season between childhood and adolescence a companion and I put on a fair of our own. My mother made lemonade, which we sold by the glass and my friend, whose father kept a livery stable, brought over two Shetland ponies, which we rented by the minute. Somebody got the idea of holding a pony race and taking bets. *Mea culpa*. Somebody fixed the race. *Mea maxima culpa*. My mother found out and ended what might have been a promising career as an impresario. God forgive us the sins of our youth. Anyhow, I've since made up for it by not cheating on my income tax. I also no longer sneak into the fair without paying.

Our Next Big Thing

I'M FOR DRINKING in moderation.

More and more of us, however, seem to be drinking to excess. I see it wherever I go. Young and old alike are turning to the bottle, and they don't even try to hide it.

I find this incredible. Not in two lifetimes could I have predicted the popularity of bottled water. Who would have dreamt that we could be inveigled into paying for it? Water is free, isn't it? Well, not exactly. But close enough that if you ask for a glass of it most anyone will give it to you without charge. Even restaurants, which are in the business of selling food and drink, give away water. So do agencies that install public drinking fountains. So, for that matter, do hotels, which charge the same for a room no matter how many showers you take.

Yet, increasing numbers of us tote around bottles of water that we paid for, and guzzle continuously in plain sight. It's a wonder more of us don't drown. It's surprising some of us aren't trampled in the rush to find public rest rooms.

It used to be that we carried water only when hiking or driving in remote areas, and we didn't buy it in bottles from a store. We collected it in jugs from a tap, ours or someone else's. Now, many of us carry store-bought water everywhere.

I can only guess why. Maybe we seek status and consider that drinking from a common tap is beneath us. Maybe we vote with our thirst, and patronize private venders over public utilities to make a political point. Maybe we worry about sanitation, and think that bottled water from a clean store is purer than tap water from a dirty well or river. Maybe we need to lose weight and believe that calorie-free water is lighter than calorie-rich food. It isn't, not if you squeeze the water out of the food.

Whatever the reasons, bottled water provides protective cover for other libations. I used to carry a concealed flask to various public spectacles and imbibe discreetly to avoid detection by unsympathetic authorities. Now, I carry an unconcealed plastic bottle and drink openly whenever the spirits move me. I blend right in.

Some enterprising folks process and bottle water at home. They install equipment that subjects ordinary tap water to such indignities as ultraviolet sterilization, deionization, reverse osmosis, and distillation. My hope is that distillation prevails. It provides protective cover for home-based production of other thirst quenchers the authorities don't want me to distil.

The sources of store-bought water are promoted as fresh, pure, cool, natural, inaccessible, exclusive. Our thirst is piqued by references to deep artesian wells, desert oases, snow-capped mountain streams, glacial springs, crystal falls, rain-fed lagoons. No wonder increasing numbers of us are driven to drink.

The last time I checked, water made up nearly seventy percent of our body weight. With all the commercialized guzzling going on, I suspect the percentage is rising. I don't know at what point the guzzlers dissolve, but I want to be around when it happens. I'd like to watch them percolate into the earth or bubble off toward the sea. I think it would be educational.

The Greek philosopher Thales said that everything comes from water. Thales was all wet. If he had said that everyone turns into water, he might have been closer to the truth.

Bottled water is a multi-billion dollar a year industry. I missed a lucrative business opportunity by not foreseeing it. But I won't be caught out when the next big thing comes along. I expect the next big thing will be bottled air. It's already popular with deep sea divers and space walkers. With the right promotion, everyone will be clamouring to breathe it.

Soon, we'll be exposed to copy like this:

Why depend on a fickle atmosphere to meet your breathing needs when you can carry your very own supply of Super Fresh Polar Air? (trade mark pending). Compressed in pristine antarctic caverns, Super Fresh Polar Air has never been breathed, not even by penguins. Get yourself a bottle today. Then charge up your hemoglobin and give your lungs a treat. Once you've tried Super Fresh Polar Air, you'll agree with countless other satisfied customers that the atmosphere is for the birds.

For a limited time only, our introductory offer provides two breaths for the price of one. Super Fresh Polar Air is certified. So are we.

Home Cooking

WHEN I WAS GROWING UP on the prairies, we seemed to be overrun with gophers. They gorged on grasses, gobbled up grain, and filled the fields with holes that threatened to break the legs of unwary livestock. Those cute little rodents were such a nuisance the government put a price on their heads. Well, actually, it was on their tails. For every gopher you killed, you qualified for a bounty, but you had to deliver the tail to collect. This was a boon to penniless urchins like me, who delivered tails by the bushel.

I don't know what the government did with all those tails. Rumour had it that government cooks removed the hair, fried up the naked tails with butter and onions, and fed them to inmates of public institutions. I don't put much stock in the rumour. Governments usually aren't that imaginative.

Come to think of it, I don't know what the gophers did with the tails, either. They were too short to swish flies with, too light to use as a rudder and too weak to swing by. Frankly, they were an embarrassment, a vestigial organ like the appendix, which the little critters were probably better off without.

We used to catch them alive, prune them on the spot, and set them free to breed. We had enough biology to know that acquired characteristics are not inherited and the offspring would arrive complete with tails to ensure our future income. Gophers are very prolific. A mother gopher can bear as many as a dozen babies each year. We didn't want to do anything to interfere with that potential cash flow. This meant that we couldn't poison, drown, shoot or club our benefactors. We had to lasso them.

We used a small diameter cord with a noose at one end and us at the other. We would lay the noose, hidden under dirt and leaves, around the perimeter of one of the holes leading to a gopher's underground quarters. When the occupant poked its head out to see what the weather was like, we snared it.

We hadn't yet learned that gopher is the common name for Richardson's ground squirrel. It's a good thing, too, because we wouldn't have known how to get Richardson's permission for what we were doing with his property. I still don't know. More important, I don't know how Richardson came into possession of all those gophers and their descendents. If I had been Richardson, I would have posted no hunting signs and harvested the tails myself. We met quite a few people while we were on gopher hole stakeouts, but never Richardson. I guess he was an absentee landlord.

When I recall those halcyon days, my entrepreneurial juices start flowing. Today, domesticating and marketing indigenous species for food is big business. Look what's happening with elk and bison. Because they're native to the prairies, they're much more economical to raise than immigrant species like cattle, swine or sheep. No animal is more indigenous to the prairies than gophers. If their tails suggest a tasty hors d'oeuvre, think what the rest of them might offer as a main course. Gophers are popular fare for weasels, coyotes, falcons and hawks. I don't see why those predators should get all the choice cuts.

Gopher colonies can be economically domesticated on less than an acre of prairie. The main requirements are above- and below-ground fencing strong and dense enough to keep the gophers in and their land-based predators out, a cover of coarse netting that admits sunshine and rain but excludes airborne predators, and supplemental rations of surplus grain to fatten the stock for marketing. Specialized facilities for slaughtering, dressing and butchering can be expected to arise through the normal workings of the economic system.

For cultural reasons, gopher meat may encounter consumer resistance. People who happily devour snails, squid and creepy crawly things like crayfish, lobster and crab turn up their noses when you offer gopher. Some who consider frog legs a delicacy consider gopher legs a disaster. I've seen it time and time again and I just don't understand why. North Americans seem far more adventurous with seafood than land food. Some who light up at the thought of pan fried shrimp throw up at the thought of fricasseed field mice. Others who calmly eat oysters raw, flee from moles no matter how they're prepared.

Clearly, we need a proper public relations program to counter this irrational behaviour. As a first step, I propose we seek a government grant to develop a recipe book with dishes calculated to please the most fastidious palate, things like ground squirrel scampi, gopher cacciatore, rack of Richardson's, and rodent stroganoff.

As an example, I offer the following for inclusion in the first edition:

CURRIED GOPHER

2 lbs. cubed lean gopher; 2 tsp. curry powder; 1/4 cup flour; 2 tbsp. shortening; 1 can (10 ounces) condensed onion soup; 1/2 soup can water; 1 cup sliced celery; 1 tart red apple cubed; 1/4 cup seedless raisins; hot cooked rice; chutney; shredded coconut; chopped peanuts

Combine flour and curry powder and roll gopher in it. Brown gopher in shortening in frying pan and blend in any remaining flour. Add soup, water, celery, apple, and raisins. Cook covered over low heat 1 hour, or until gopher is tender. Stir often during cooking. Serve over hot rice (about 4 cups cooked). Garnish with chutney, coconut, and peanuts. Makes 6 to 8 servings.

SUGGESTED WINES

Dandelion is the first choice, provided the plants have reached maturity in close proximity to gopher colonies. Otherwise, any wine fermented from indigenous sources will splendidly complement this tasty dish.

Gophers are but one of many indigenous species that we might profitably raise for food. Others which are highly recommended include porcupines, partly because they provide their own toothpicks; cougars, because if we don't eat them they might eat us; and groundhogs, because few dishes are more appealing than a roast suckling groundhog with a crabapple in its mouth.

Hold the Phone

ALEXANDER GRAHAM BELL had a good idea, but modern technology has ruined it. Scientific wizardry has taken the mystery out of the telephone. The electronics revolution has removed the romance. Computer nerds have eliminated the fun.

We used to be able to phone up Mrs. Cherry and ask if she was ripe yet. We can't do that anymore. Today, Mrs. Cherry probably has call display or, worse still, name display.

Occasionally, we would get a wrong connection and spend a few exciting moments chatting with a mysterious stranger of the opposite sex. We can't anonymously do that anymore, either.

Oh, I know the new technology has its defenders. It's supposed to make it easier to locate swindlers who use the phones for fraud or lechers who make obscene calls. But I don't want to locate swindlers or lechers. If I did, I'd put an ad in the personal section of the local paper. You'd be surprised what people advertise for nowadays.

I hate getting a recorder when I phone people. I can visualize them spread-eagled in front of the television set, letting the calls pile up and deciding which ones not to return. That's why I rarely leave messages. I keep calling until someone, not a machine, answers. If I left a message, I suspect it would be a nasty one. I'm afraid I would say something like, "Pick up the phone, cheese head. I know you're sitting there vegetating."

Not everyone leaves the recorder on while at home. Some do only when they go out. But all too often they forget to check for messages after they return, or choose not to acknowledge mine. Recorders give the receiver an unfair advantage over the sender.

Even worse, though, are the disembodied voices you reach when you try to get information through a touch-tone phone. Responding to their instructions can be both confusing and stressful. You can't get them to explain anything. They neither laugh nor cry. It's like shaking hands with a shadow. I liked it better when there was less information but more living, breathing people to provide it. It was a challenge to penetrate their professional reserve. It was fun to amuse or annoy them. Now there's neither hilarity nor exasperation, just indifference.

But computer technology has made it easier and relatively inexpensive to phone all over the world. You can access disembodied voices from Austria to Zimbabwe. You can insult computers from Mexico to Morocco. Yes, I insult computers whenever I get the chance. Computers infuriate me, especially when they talk to me. They're so smug and aloof. If they could think, they'd think they were superior to us mortals. Of course, they can't think. They only think they can.

But beneath their superficial, mathematical sorcery, they're really quite dumb. There's not an ounce of creativity in a ton of electronics. Letting computers take over the phones is like letting the marionettes take over the puppet show. We made them. They didn't make us, even though they act as though we couldn't exist without them. So the next time you encounter a computer consider a snide remark, a vulgar gesture, a common assault. Computers deserve no less.

The days when the telephone could bring unanticipated adventure are long gone. The times when it could inspire composers to write love songs are no more. There's nothing adventurous about computers. They're programmed. There's nothing to inspire a song writer in disembodied voices. They lack flesh and blood. No one gets sentimental over telephone numbers nowadays. They're much too long, they change too often, and there are too many add-ons, like area codes for long distance and all manner of digits for specialized services.

But it wasn't always this way. I still get nostalgic over the shorter numbers of yesteryear. When I think of 97093, the five digit number I grew up with in the 1930s, I can smell cookies baking in a small kitchen and I can see a kindly auburn haired lady, my mother, gossiping happily on the phone with one of her bridge friends. I get embarrassingly emotional about our tiny house and big lot with all kinds of trees for climbing and our next door neighbour coming over to make a call because she didn't have a phone of her own. When I think of 97408, the number at a house up the street, I see a little girl with ringlets coming down the front steps and running toward me. It's been a depressingly long time since a girl has run toward me.

In those days, phones used to ring. Now they trill demandingly like hypertensive waterfowl. I believe they're programmed to stimulate some obscure hormone that prompts us to come to the aid of strangers in distress. Every time the phone trills my blood pressure rises alarmingly and I get apprehensive. I feel terribly guilty if I don't answer, as if I'd let someone down who really needed me.

Not all the options they boast about nowadays are new. They make a fuss over conference calls. Well, we had party lines more than half a century ago. Every household had its own ring, but anyone on the line could listen in and usually did. It was one of the chief means of disseminating news. We may not have had speaker phones or intercoms, but we shouted a lot and never missed them.

I guess cell phones are what disturb me most. You hear people chatting away on them in the supermarket, at the restaurant, in the theatre. It's intrusive and distracting. It's especially distracting when they get calls in Church. With all the praying and singing, I have trouble listening in on what they're saying. Some people have them in their cars. That can cause accidents. Others use them in public rest rooms, keeping me waiting until they finish talking. That can cause accidents, too.

I've resisted virtually all the new features. I did weaken and buy a cordless phone, however. It was a mistake. I carry it with me always. I feel vulnerable without it, on the patio, in the garden, taking out the garbage. I never used to worry about missing calls or having to hurry to respond to a distant phone. Now, when the batteries in my portable are being recharged, I worry about it constantly. It's dreadful. It is as though I were wired into a vast electronics network, a kind of universal mind, with no space for individuality. My only hope is to smash the portable and join Gabbers Anonymous.

Have I Got News for You

I USED TO BE A TELEVISION NEWSCASTER. It's not something I'm especially proud of. It was a job and I needed the money. I worked at it during the early years of television, before computer graphics, before videotape, even before colour. We did have sound, though.

As I recall, we didn't smile much while telecasting. We didn't frown much either. We were a pretty deadpan lot. We stuck to the script. The only time we ad-libbed was when we misplaced an item and had to convey the information somehow. We had some quaint idea that we were supposed to be reporters, not editorialists, interpreters or, heaven forbid, entertainers. The information we delivered was central, the medium peripheral. The message was the end. We were the means. It never occurred to us that this might be bad for our self-esteem.

People recognized us on the street, but they didn't think of us as television personalities. We had a peculiar effect on them, nonetheless. Ten years after I left the job, a stranger approached me and said, "I haven't seen you on the news lately. Have you been on assignment?"

Television news is different now. Nowadays, the medium is a significant part of the message. The newscasters are all celebrities. They don't just report the news. They participate in it. They seem concerned that we'll misunderstand, misinterpret or misapply the facts. So they make faces at us. Happy faces, sad faces, worried faces, perplexed faces, disgusted faces. With these, and a similar range of vocal gymnastics, they guide us in meaning. It's wonderful. We don't have to think for ourselves anymore.

They seem convinced that they need to form some kind of relationship with us. So the newscasters, sportscasters and weather men, or women, chat away at us as if they were part of the family. At the end of the news, sports and weather, they exchange inanities, just like family members, and reveal intimate trivialities, just like real people. They obviously believe that news is dull, and they have to smarten it up, information is bleak and they have to brighten it up, facts are cold and they have to warm them up, we're unhappy and they have to cheer us up.

I detect a woman's touch in all of this. Feminists tell us that women are better than men at relationships. I believe they're right. It never occurred to us pioneer newscasters to try to form a relationship with our viewers. As long as they understood us, we didn't care much whether they loved us. We had some Neanderthal notion that in this context the stories were more important than our personalities, the facts were more significant than our opinion of them. No doubt, the absence of women had something to do with our lack of sensitivity. There weren't any women newscasters in those days. Or if there were, I didn't know of them. Either television discriminated against women or women discriminated against television. I'm not sure which.

Whatever it was, it's all changed now. Women are everywhere. Whether or not it did then, television news doesn't discriminate against women now. It just discriminates against ugly women. You can see ugly male newscasters anytime. Ugly female newscasters are a rarity, if they exist at all. On a scale of one to ten, the females congregate at the upper levels.

The feminist movement ought to do something about this. You've got to hand it to the feminists. They don't discriminate against ugly women. The movement is full of them. They even get to fill the top positions. Let's give credit where credit is due. But let's hope that the feminists bring about a little balance in television news and replace some of the tens with a representative number of ones. Some kind of affirmative action would seem to be in order.

Celebrity reporters go to great lengths to participate in the stories they cover. I'm thinking especially of Melanie Trew, who is regularly featured on my favourite news channel. All smiles and flashing eyes, Ms Trew has a nose for the kind of news she can demonstrate. So if it's sky diving, marathon bicycling, pie-eating contests or first aid courses, the anchor will regale us with something like: And here's our own Melanie Trew, soaring like an eagle, pedalling her legs off, stuffing her face, or trussed up like a mummy.

Ms Trew's fearlessness and versatility are marvelous to behold. I can't wait until they assign her to cover a riot, a drug bust or a roundup of street walkers. I can imagine the anchor's introduction: And here's our own Melanie Trew looting a store, snorting cocaine or soliciting on Second Avenue.

Maybe they feel that they have to compete with the commercials. When I was in television, newscasts were a commercial-free zone. You could slot commercials around the news but never in the midst of it. That's all changed now, too. Nowadays, we can watch four, five or six commercials without the interruption of a single news item. This, no doubt, is why some telecasters sound like promoters. To keep up with the commercials, they don't just present the news, they sell it.

This also may explain their stylishness. To look rumpled or wrinkled after a commercial on the latest fashions might cause viewers to make invidious comparisons. So newscasters, the women especially, dress to the nines and pour on the makeup. It was much simpler in my day. In the absence of colour, we could be colourless. In a commercial-free zone, we could dress down without attracting attention.

Recently, the TV station I worked at celebrated an anniversary and invited me to attend. The advances I saw are truly breathtaking. One of the biggest changes is in how they do the weather. In my day, the weather forecast was no big deal. We just sort of tacked it on at the end of the news. Today, it's a major production. We had a few primitive graphics and we often got the forecast wrong. Today, everything's state of the art, and they still get it wrong, only more professionally.

I guess professionalism is the real difference between then and now. We got hired, most of us, right off the street, as they say. Today's telecasters are graduates of prestigious journalism schools, where they learn how to form relationships with their viewers, make faces at them, engage in small talk, look pretty, slant the news, create the stories they report, and fool everyone into thinking they can predict the weather. I certainly did miss out.

My Annual Food Fight

A HARBINGER OF SPRING is the first sighting of my tax assessment notice peeping out of the mail box. It's uncannily prophetic. A harbinger of fall is the first arrival of garden produce on my back step. It's uncannily prophetic, too. Neither the tax collectors who drain me nor the gardeners who overwhelm me take no for an answer. To them, no means yes.

I don't garden. I've never had any success at it. I suspect that plants dislike me. But I'm surrounded by gardeners, friends and neighbours who are all thumbs, green thumbs. During the growing season, gardening is the only thing they seem to do and the only topic they want to discuss. Since I don't know a zucchini from a Zamboni, I just listen. I listen, but I don't learn.

Sooner or later, the gardens ripen and their owners are surprised to discover that they have far more produce than they can eat, process or store. Every year they make the same surprising discovery. That's when the fruit and vegetables start piling up on my back step, and I, too, have more produce than I can eat, process or store, only I'm not surprised.

As soon as I receive my tax assessment notice, I warn the gardeners about planting too much. They listen, but like me they don't learn. At harvest time, I'm tempted to say "I told you so." I don't bother. I save my strength for coping with their surplus.

I also don't want to hurt their feelings. Gardeners have sensitive feelings, especially at harvest time. They grow their gardens with as much tender loving care as they rear their children. Harvest time is like high school or university graduation, when they send their little darlings into the world and bask in the reflected glory. I just wish that when they dig, pull and pick their produce they wouldn't see me as a doting recipient and expect me to glorify their carrots, which I can't stand raw, their spinach, which I can't stand cooked, their crabapples, which I can't stand unjellied, and their zucchinis, which I can't stand at all.

For a few weeks each year I become a vegetarian. This helps, but not much. No matter how diligently I work at it, I can't consume more than a small fraction of what they send me, not without injuring myself. As for processing and storage, I've long since run out of recipes and room. Since I'd surely be found out if I gave or threw the stuff away in the neighbourhood, I wait for a moonless night and spirit it off to a local soup kitchen.

I've had other ideas about disposing of orphan food, but I lack the initiative to carry them out. I've thought about composting it and giving it to the neighbourhood gardeners as fertilizer the following spring. I wouldn't, of course, tell them that I was returning their produce recycled. I've thought about gift wrapping choice items and using them to tip the paper boy and the mailman for substandard service. I could do the same with the obsequious waiters who hover over me in some of the local restaurants and lounges.

Mostly, though, I've thought about drying, waxing, laminating or embalming my unsought produce and turning it into art objects or holiday decorations. I've fantasized about sculpting the faces of friends and neighbours on the huge turnips they foist on me and fastening them to my roof like gargoyles or hanging them from my eaves like shrunken heads. If you can create art out of raw meat, as is alleged to have been done, why not out of raw vegetables?

I've fantasized about stringing the trees in my front yard with grotesque baubles fashioned from my benefactors' misshapen potatoes, wreaths from their wilted beet tops, festoons from their carrots and cucumbers, garlands from their lettuce and spinach, interspersed with their cherry tomatoes and plums. I've imagined myself building lawn furniture out of their swollen melons and inviting them to sit in it.

You'd think that they could ferment all that vegetation into wine or distil it into hard liquor. That's the kind of processing I could relate to and the kind of product I'd be content to receive on my back step anytime. In the meantime, I've been hinting that they should supplement their gardening with aquaculture. I'm open to regular shipments of rainbow trout, tiger shrimp, scallops and muscles. They'd go well with the liquor and wine.

Should none of this happen, I have a plan that just might spare me future vegetative invasions. Although I don't garden, I'm not without hobbies. I compose music and write poetry and essays. Whenever friends and neighbours try to ditch their produce on my back step, I intend to invite them in and insist that they listen to me perform my songs and give readings of my literary works.

Like them, I won't take no for an answer. Like me, they'll be looking for a way out. The easiest way is to cross me off their gift lists. Then they can haul the produce to the soup kitchen themselves.

Down with Renown

FAMOUS PEOPLE fluster me. I shouldn't go near them. I always say or do the wrong thing. When he appeared in our town, I was introduced to comedian Dave Broadfoot. I asked him if he was related to singer Gordon Lightfoot. I couldn't help it. I felt that I had to say something and that's what came out. I was so befuddled it seemed a reasonable question to ask. My emotions, mainly panic, had taken over and my mind was on hold.

Trying to locate a piece of misplaced luggage at the Toronto airport, I found myself beside a distinguished looking blonde in the same predicament. It was Joni Mitchell, known in some quarters as the first lady of rock. I tried to appear nonchalant, not letting on that I knew who she was. It was no use. I could no longer concentrate on my lost bags and began to hum distractedly — not one of her songs, one of my songs. No one but me has performed any of my songs. I couldn't help myself. The longer I went on, the more rattled I got. Fortunately, her luggage appeared before I collapsed in a fit nervous exhaustion and she left, bringing an abrupt end to the audition.

I ran into Louis Armstrong, literally, when he was performing in Saskatoon. I was hurrying to the rest room at intermission and we collided behind the bandstand. Anyone else would have said, "Pardon me" or "So sorry."

I gasped, "I play the trumpet, too." Don't ask me why I said that. Although I do happen to play the trumpet, it was beside the point. Meeting the greatest name in jazz must have overloaded my circuits. I don't recall what, if anything, he said in reply. I know for certain that he didn't invite me to sit in with the band.

The first celebrities I saw in person were King George VI and Queen Elizabeth during their 1939 Royal Visit to Canada. I was part of a troop of cubs (junior boy scouts) lining one of the streets on the royal route. As their open convertible approached, the Queen looking elegant and stately, the King looking bored and out of sorts, I started hyperventilating and the next thing I knew I was on my knees. A couple of elderly women waving tiny Union Jacks shouted "God save the King." They must have thought I was leading them in prayer, so I yelled "amen". Some of my saucy friends chimed in with "hallelujah." A policeman guarding our part of the route took me aside and scolded me. He said I was causing a disturbance and could wake the King up.

A few years later, when some friends and I boarded a streetcar, the only seat I could find was beside John Diefenbaker. In those days, members of Parliament were apt to show up anywhere. We had no idea who he was and totally ignored him as we joshed and jibed the way adolescents do. Someone discreetly informed one of my companions, who proceeded to display a strange repertoire of gesticulations and facial contortions aimed at revealing the identity of my seat mate to me. The rest joined in, mouthing the MP's name and pointing.

In response, I looked Mr. Diefenbaker full in the face and the blood drained from my head. I was, of course, speechless and lacking in all social graces. Without realizing it, I slid to the edge of the seat. Eventually, I slid right off, ending up sitting on the floor, while Mr. Diefenbaker, looking like a caricature of himself, glanced down at me unperturbed. Mercifully, the streetcar soon came to a stop, his stop, and I regained the seat, all of it. I can only wonder how much worse it might have been if I'd known he was destined to become Prime Minister.

When I was a young reporter, the Archbishop of Canterbury came to town to do the honours at a sod turning ceremony for a new Anglican church. The news editor assigned me to cover the story. It's not often that such a prestigious personage appears in the middle of the Canadian prairies and I was visibly shaken. I went anyway. I had a soft spot in my heart for Canterbury because of Geoffrey Chaucer's *The Canterbury Tales*, my favourite book from 1385. Or was it 1386? The archbishop handled the shovel well and gave a passable speech. By the time I got back to the newsroom, I thought I had largely overcome my fear of fame and boldly headed the story: Archbishop Turns Sod.

"We can't say that." the editor shouted. "We don't even know if he drinks."

I guess the fame I'm most uncomfortable with is my own. Although not in a class with any of the aforementioned, I have occasionally achieved a modest notoriety, locally and even regionally. It first happened when I became a television newscaster. All sorts of people I didn't know seemed to know me. Some of them stared at me, even pointed at me, in public. Others greeted me by name and tried to engage me in conversation. Still others scolded me because I'd misled them about the weather. They held me personally responsible.

I put up with it for five years, but it took its toll. I felt that I didn't totally belong to myself, that hordes of outsiders somehow owned a piece of me. I was relieved when other employment became available. I assumed that once I withdrew from public life, the stalkers and harassers would turn their attention elsewhere. I was wrong. For years, I had to field such questions as "Have you been on assignment?", "Are you taking a leave of absence?", "How long will you be working behind the scenes?", "Is the rain going to hold off for my barbecue tomorrow?"

A few years later, in the heyday of the Beatles, a friend and I started a dixieland jazz band. Starting a dixieland band in the heyday of the Beatles was like starting a livery stable in the heyday of the Ford Mustang. For reasons I don't pretend to understand, it worked. Otherwise normal people actually paid to hear us. While everyone else was singing "With A Little Help From My Friends", we were playing "Basin Street Blues" and getting away with it. The only problem was that we became somewhat popular, slightly famous. Once again, limited though it was, I had to cope with notoriety. I was a known trumpeter.

The day after one of our concerts, a complete stranger stopped me in the street and asked, "At the end of the final number, was that a high C you hit?"

"No," I replied, "that was the trombone player I hit. He was talking during my chorus."

It was a rude response, I know, but it embarrassed me to discuss my range in public. It still does. The same goes for my swoops, glides, glisses and smears. I don't even discuss them in private. It's a matter of musical etiquette. That didn't stop determined jazz buffs, however. They expected me to tell all. Some of them asked pointedly personal questions about my lower register. Others wanted to know if I practised breath control.

The media interviewers were especially intrusive. They insisted on talking about the theory underlying our polyphonic improvisation. I couldn't even pronounce it much less analyze it.

Eventually, we appeared on local television.

"I caught you the other night," a fan told me a few days later. "When did they start accompanying your newscasts with music?"

Modern Philosophy

HE LOVES TO ARGUE. Mostly he loves to argue about the big questions, like why is there something rather than nothing. Rarely does he agree about anything. Indeed, he dislikes agreeing. It stops him from arguing.

I remember one day trying to convince him that everything is what it is.

"On the contrary," he said, "everything is only what it appears to be."

"You mean that everything is relative?"

"Absolutely."

"But if everything is relative," I said, "our knowledge is relative, too, and we can't know anything for sure."

"Certainly not," he replied.

"Then what's the point of talking? If reality and our knowledge of it are as you say, we can debate endlessly and never hope to agree."

"I concur," he said with conviction.

"In other words, we're doomed always to doubt?"

"Indubitably."

"And truth is unattainable."

"Truly."

I tried a different tack.

"You must admit," I said, "that things exist outside the mind."

"I admit nothing."

"But if there is no objective reality, if everything is subjective, communication is impossible."

"I see we understand each other."

"Perhaps nothing exists, including us."

"I didn't say that."

"I know you didn't, but when you sink into such subjectivism, how can you establish your own existence?

"I sink, therefore I am."

It was comforting to know that he existed, but I was worried about his ethics.

"Without objective standards," I said, "morality is meaningless."

"Standards are against my principles," he replied.

"Then you must hold that there can be no such thing as right and wrong.

"Right."

"Good and evil are essentially indistinguishable."

"Good."

"Our universe is both metaphysically and ethically vague."

"Precisely."

How, I wondered, could society survive such moral individualism?

"You seem to deny the fundamental bases of law and order," I said.

"I'm not a fundamentalist."

"I would never accuse you of that. What I mean is you seem to reject natural law."

"Naturally."

"I'm afraid that your philosophy is a recipe for anarchy."

"I'm not an anarchist. I just feel that we each have a right to do our own thing."

"Yes, but one person's rights are another's duties. You can't have one without the other," I said confidantly. "You can't choose between them." I thought I had him.

"That may be so logically, but not emotionally. Nowadays, emotion is a higher force than reason. What we feel is more important than what we know. I choose rights. They feel better than duties."

I could see that my approach was getting me nowhere. I had been appealing to reason. Perhaps I should appeal to faith.

"What religion do you dissent from?"

"I'm not religious."

"You don't believe in God?"

"Heaven forbid."

"Then you certainly don't believe in damnation."

"Hell no!"

"Do you believe in anything?" I asked, desperately.

"I believe in nothing."

"Then you don't believe in anything."

"On the contrary, I believe in nothing."

"But nothing doesn't exist. If you believe in nothing, you don't believe in anything."

He shook his head gravely.

"Although nothing doesn't exist," he said, "it nevertheless is. Otherwise we wouldn't be able to talk about it."

"You seem to be saying that nothing is something. Indeed, it may even be the ultimate reality."

"Now you're getting the idea."

"But surely you can't be serious. If what is, or is not, is as you suggest, the universe is absurd, life is a joke, and we're ridiculous."

He looked troubled.

"I think we should end this discussion," he said.

"Why should we do that?"

"You're beginning to agree with me."

Under the Weather and Over the Hill

SINCE BECOMING what is euphemistically called a senior citizen, I qualify for all sorts of perks and favours. It's society's final attempt at undermining my independence. The federal government is leading the charge. As soon as I reached the arbitrarily designated age, the government granted me a significant pension. At the same time, it issued me a plastic card proclaiming that I'm in receipt of a benefit under the Old Age Security Act and asking that I be extended all possible privileges. As soon as I read that, I went to see my banker.

"Are you aware," I said, waving the card. "that I'm a certified old guy?"

He was non-committal.

"Did you know," I said, "that the federal government wants you to extend to me all possible privileges?" If he knew, he wasn't letting on.

"If you could possibly lend me a hundred thousand dollars interest free," I continued, "the federal government would like you to do so." He seemed quietly annoyed. Maybe he had wanted to surprise me and the government was upstaging him.

I told him that if for any reason he withheld the money the government would be disappointed.

"Are you prepared to live with that?" I asked.

Apparently, he was. He invited me and the government to step aside while he served the next client.

But most people find my seniority irresistible. I don't even have to flash the plastic card. No sooner do I board a bus than frail young women jump to their feet and offer me their places. I always decline. Such unsolicited bids suggest that I'm even frailer than they are. Besides, if I accept one, I have to reject the others. That could be dangerous nowadays. In retaliation, I tell them I'd rather sit on their laps, all of them. This usually dispels any chivalrous impulses, and they settle for treating me with studied indifference.

Other well-meaning souls assume that I'm half deaf, legally blind, mentally compromised and financially stressed. They shout when they talk to me, foist large-print books on me, explain things to me endlessly, and insist on giving me discounts on goods and services. It's enough to make me want to be young again.

One of the benefits of being young is that you are unlikely to be called a junior citizen. I've been accused of many things, but not that. But if I've never been a junior, how did I suddenly become a senior? To be a senior implies that at one time or another I was a junior. Maybe I'm not a senior citizen after all.

I sometimes pretend I'm not. Once in a while I try to pass as an uncertified old guy. It doesn't work. Too many people know me. They keep asking how I like retirement.

"It's what I've always wanted to do," I invariably reply.

They think I'm being facetious, but I was never more serious. I wanted to retire as soon as I started to work. When my wife and I were raising a family, our wants outstripped our finances. Now, with multiple pensions and accumulated savings, our finances outstrip our wants, not to mention our capacity to consume. Does that make sense to you? It doesn't to me. We should retire when we're young enough to exploit it and work when we're too old to care. That's what I plan to do next time.

Of course, I'm not your typical retiree. Most people slow down as they grow older. I don't. I slow up. It's more challenging. Many get ugly. Not me. I was ugly to begin with. Many others lose their resilience. I never had any. I couldn't afford it. Still others become unsociable. I don't as long as I'm left alone.

They say that as we age we decline in intelligence, but you couldn't prove it by me. I have no comparative data. I cheated on the IQ tests. I didn't want my teachers to know how bright I was, or wasn't. I was afraid they'd expect more from me than I was ready to give. Consequently, I'll never know whether I'm getting smarter or dumber, not if I live until I'm an idiot.

One thing I have in common with other seniors is aches and pains. If nothing else, growing old hurts. With some of us there are more pains than aches, with others just the reverse. Whatever the proportion, they're great conversation starters. Often they not only start the conversation, they sustain it, indefinitely. Unless you've got the day off, the first rule in approaching seniors is never to ask how they are.

The older I get, the more popular I become with doctors, druggists and morticians. They suspect that sooner or later I'll require their expensive services. I suppose it's possible to escape the doctors and druggists. The morticians are another matter. Unless I expire by spontaneous combustion, they'll no doubt get to cremate me, bury me, or stuff me. The latter option is tempting. When I was a boy I wanted to join the RCMP. I got sidetracked into journalism. But if in life I failed to become a mounted policeman, it's comforting to think that in death I could become a mounted police reporter.

Bowing Out

MARK TWAIN WAS RIGHT. It's bad form to face death without having your last words ready. Twain was referring to the last words of great men. He wasn't talking about ordinary folks like you and me. He wasn't even talking about great women. Maybe he didn't know any great women.

Anyhow, it seems to me that greatness is beside the point. In the information age, we all need to have our last words ready. Nowadays, death can be as embarrassing without appropriate last words as without a proper will. There's no excuse for it. With an unprecedented ability to record, store, retrieve and transmit data, we should all be able to prepare our last words ahead of time and go out in style.

What got me thinking this way was a medical emergency. Early one morning, I reacted badly to a drug my doctor had prescribed and collapsed unconscious on the bathroom floor. It was a new experience for me, and when I came to I thought I might be on the brink of eternity. My wife evidently thought the same and called 911. The paramedics arrived within minutes, took my pulse and blood pressure, connected me to an oxygen tank, started an I.V. drip, and whisked me off to the hospital in an ambulance.

I recovered quickly and was able to return home in a cab a couple of hours later. But it could have been serious, because I hadn't prepared any last words. I still blush when I think of it. Imagine if I'd been at death's door and blurted out some mundane thing like "Call the drug store and demand a refund," or "Send the doctor the bill for the ambulance." To sign off on such an uninspiring note would have been indefensible. But I had nothing better to say and in all the medical confusion my mind wasn't working as well as usual.

It was then I realized that last words should be conceived and rehearsed in good health. Only in this way can we hope to ensure a sterling and dignified departure. If we wait too long, we risk making an uncivilized exit and embarrassing not only ourselves but our family and friends. Even worse, we may be tempted to plagiarize the last words of our literary betters and go into eternity in disgrace.

The important thing about last words is that they are likely to last. People tend to remember them. So if for want of preparation you say something trivial or foolish, it will humiliate your descendants for generations. On the other hand, if you prepare something edifying and original, it will comfort and inspire them until the seed runs out.

Once you've come up with something fitting, the temptation to use it ahead of time is almost irresistible. But resist it you must. Look what happened to William Shakespeare. He created a splendid exit line in "To be or not to be — that is the question" and gave it to Hamlet. Instead of going out with a flourish, Shakespeare died in relative obscurity, which caused some critics to attribute his plays to Christopher Marlowe or Francis Bacon, who presumably saved their best lines until the end.

John Donne squandered " . . . never send to know for whom the bell tolls; it tolls for thee" on one of his metaphysical poems, and went into his final agony tongue tied. If only he'd had the discipline to save it for a grand finale, Ernest Hemingway would never have stolen part of it for one of his novels. He wouldn't have dared.

Then there's Marie Antoinette. She went down in history as a compassionate ruler when she allegedly invited her subjects for dessert. But instead of wasting "Let them eat cake" on the French revolution, she should have saved it for her demise, and gone up in history.

More recently, Winston Churchill prematurely tossed off "Never in the field of human conflict was so much owed by so many to so few." As last words, they could have resonated down the ages. Uttered in the heat of World War Two, they've already lost much of their meaning and hardly anyone remembers that Churchill was complaining about the national debt.

You can be sure that Neil Armstrong, the first person to set foot on the moon, will never forgive himself for failing to keep "That's one small step for man, one giant leap for mankind" to usher him into the next world. He missed the opportunity of a death time.

On the other hand, Sir Thomas More saved his best words for the last, eloquently petitioning his executioner to spare his beard when he chopped off his head. It was a magnificent exit, and they made him a saint.

John Brown also bowed out in glory. Before his body began mouldering in the grave, he announced that he was as content "to die for God's eternal truth on the scaffold as in any other way." Despite the difficulties with his body, his soul went marching on, and we've been singing about it for a century and a half. It shows you how powerful a proper set of last words can be.

Even a single last word can be electrifying, if it's the right one. George Gershwin was heard to mumble "Astaire" as he lapsed into the coma that preceded his death. By associating himself with the classy Fred Astaire and his incomparable dancing, Gershwin consolidated his place in the annals of American music. It was a brilliant coup and well planned. But it was risky. Imagine if he had mumbled "Ebsen" instead. Buddy Ebsen, another contemporary dancer, ended up as a *Beverly Hillbilly*. In view of the risks, single last words are not generally recommended.

You might protest that ordinary folks can't be expected to come up with extraordinary lines. Nonsense. Most anyone can create at least one good epigram in a lifetime, just as most anyone can produce at least one good joke. The secret is to start early. You should begin thinking about your last words as soon as possible after uttering your first words. If, after years of trying, nothing comes to mind, you can always hire a ghost writer. No one needs to know.

Once you've settled on something, commit it to memory and leave it there. Except for private rehearsals, don't even think of bringing it out until you're ready to depart. Timing is everything. If you speak too soon, you might recover and look absurd. If you wait too long, you might be unable to speak and appear negligent. Last words spoken up to twenty-four hours ahead are acceptable. Anything earlier is questionable; anything later is usually impossible. Insist that the doctor give you his best estimate of the time remaining. If he underestimates, sue him. Not for money, for another set of last words, as you will have used yours prematurely. If he overestimates, your executors can sue him.

Without medical help, General James Wolfe spoke his last words within the twenty-four hour grace period. On the eve of battle, he said of Gray's famous *Elegy*, "I'd rather have written those lines than take Quebec." Well, he didn't get his wish. He took Quebec in spite of himself and was mortally wounded doing it. Before passing on, he declared, "Now God be praised. I will die in peace." He died in peace because he'd got off a pretty good set of last words.